Inviting
Educational
Leadership

SCHOOL LEADERSHIP AND MANAGEMENT SERIES

Series Editors: Brent Davies and John West-Burnham

Inviting Educational Leadership

Fulfilling potential and applying an ethical perspective to the educational process

John M. Novak

London · New York · Toronto · Sydney · Tokyo
Singapore · Hong Kong · Cape Town · New Delhi · Madrid
Paris · Amsterdam · Munich · Milan · Stockholm

PEARSON EDUCATION LIMITED

Head Office:
Edinburgh Gate
Harlow CM20 2JE
Tel: +44 (0)1279 623623
Fax: +44 (0)1279 431059

London Office:
128 Long Acre
London WC2E 9AN
Tel: +44 (0)20 7447 2000
Fax: +44 (0)20 7240 5771
Website: www.educationminds.com

_____

First published in Great Britain in 2002

© John M. Novak 2002

The right of John M. Novak to be identified as author
of this work has been asserted by him in accordance
with the Copyright, Designs and Patents Act 1988.

ISBN 0 273 65495 0

British Library Cataloguing in Publication Data
A CIP catalogue record for this book can be obtained from the British Library.

10 9 8 7 6 5 4 3 2 1

Typeset by Pantek Arts Ltd, Maidstone, Kent.
Printed and bound in Great Britain

The Publishers' policy is to use paper manufactured from sustainable forests.

About the Author

■ ■ ■

John M. Novak is a Professor of Education at Brock University, St Catharines, Ontario, Canada, where he has been Chair of the Department of Graduate Studies, Chair of the University Faculty Board and a member of the Board of Trustees. He received an academic scholarship and Bachelor of Arts degree in Philosophy from Ohio University, a Master of Arts degree and teacher certification from Western Carolina University, and his doctorate, combining Psychological and Social Foundations of Education, from the University of Florida. In public schools he has taught from the pre-school to the secondary school level. An active lecturer and writer, he teaches courses in educational leadership, philosophy of education, invitational education, and social and psychological foundations of education. He has won teaching awards for his work in higher education and has been a visiting professor at universities across North America, the UK and South Africa. He has also presented papers at philosophical, psychological and educational conferences throughout the world and has been an invited keynote speaker on six continents. His recent books include the third edition of *Inviting School Success* (with William Purkey), *Democratic Teacher Education, Advancing Invitational Thinking* and *Invitational Education* (with William Purkey). His forthcoming publications focus on inviting online education and creating inviting schools.

About the Series Editors

■ ■ ■

Professor Brent Davies PhD is Director of the International Leadership Centre at the University of Hull. Brent works exclusively on headteacher and senior staff development programmes in the UK and in Australia, New Zealand and the USA. He has written 11 books and published over 50 articles.

John West-Burnham is Professor of Educational Leadership, International Leadership Centre, University of Hull. John worked in schools for 15 years before moving into higher education. He has worked at Crewe and Alsager College, the University of Leicester and the University of Lincolnshire and Humberside. He was also Development Officer for Teacher Performance for Cheshire local education authority. John is author of *Managing Quality in Schools*, and co-author of *Effective Learning in Schools* and *Leadership and Professional Development in Schools*.

Acknowledgements

■ ■ ■

Books get written because invitations are extended, acknowledged, and acted upon. The invitations that have made this book possible cross several continents. In particular, I would like to acknowledge the support of the following.

In England: Brent and Barbara Davies, John West-Burnham, Amelia Lakin, Kate Lodge, and Josephine Bryan.

In South Africa: Martyn Van der Merwe and Linda MacFarlane.

In the United States: William and Imogene Purkey.

In Canada: Rahul Kumar, Thomas Busnarda, Dawn Pollon, Ken McClelland, Paul Faris, Kayli Riann, Judy Lee, Rosemary Young, and Michael Manley-Casimer.

In the Novak households: Eddy, Danny, Larry, Michael, Mabel, Richard, Adeline, Linda and Natalie.

In particular, I would like to dedicate this book to my late mother, Josephine Novak, who showed me the importance of care, play and a unique dance with life.

Contents

■ ■ ■

Introduction

■ ■ ■

This book takes the position that leadership is about people, and educational leadership is about the caring and ethical relationships between and among people, institutions and the larger society. Inviting educational leadership is about the special ethical quality of relationships needed to appreciate individuals and call forth their potential in their personal and professional lives.

At present, there is a deep-seated struggle going on for the heart of schooling. Some argue that schools should be run like businesses, with students seen as either raw material to be shaped or customers to be satisfied. Others oppose this and say it should be business as usual in schools. They feel that the schools we have are as good as they get. The way we presently do things is all we dare hope for. Although acknowledging that there are productive business practices from which educators can learn (and also practices from institutions outside the business domain), and believing that there are many current worthwhile schooling practices on which we need to build (and many from which we need to move), this book takes the position that both these perspectives are short-sighted and miss the educational heart of schooling for a democratic society.

Inviting Educational Leadership argues that the heart of schooling is schooling with an educational heart, that is headed in an educationally defensible direction, and that is coming to grips with vital educational issues. Although schooling is not the same as education, schools serve a democratic society better if they are informed by educational ideals and reflect thoughtful ethical practices. From the perspective used in this book, educators are not people who want to become bosses or bureaucrats, but caring professionals who want to lead for educational purposes, in educational ways, by inviting educational fulfilment in themselves and others.

The book is divided into three parts. The first part, 'Inviting Educational Life' is comprised of the first two chapters. The first chapter looks at what is unique about an educational perspective and the ideals that guide it. The Educational LIVES model is offered as a way to think about the relationships of an educator's life. Chapter 2 takes the position that there is nothing more practical than a good theory. It shows how an inviting approach to educational leadership has solid roots and practical possibilities. With an understanding of the democratic ethos, the perceptual tradition and self-concept theory, educational leaders can have a framework for better articulating the heart of their educational ideals. The inviting approach, however, is about more than just ideals. It is a concrete theory of practice that focuses on the quantity and quality of messages extended verbally, non-verbally, formally and informally through people, places, policies, programmes and processes. It is based on the idea that schools can intentionally invite the educational potential of all who participate in them. The inviting approach is combined with the Educational LIVES model to show that inviting educational leadership can provide a systematic way to orchestrate feelings, thoughts and actions. This model provides a basis for Part Two of this book: 'Leading and Managing Educational Life' (Chapters 3–12).

The first two chapters in Part Two look at the relationships leaders have with themselves. Chapter 3 examines personal leadership. Beginning with the idea that leaders must first be human and only after that professional, this chapter looks at the authentic commitments and personal character needed to invite educational leadership. The contention of this chapter is that educators need to be committed to living an educational life if they are seeking to lead others to do so. This involves an examination of intentional behaviour – doing things on purpose for purposes that can be defended. Chapter 4 takes seriously the idea that if you do not take care of yourself in the present, you are not going to be an educational leader in the long run. Some nuts-and-bolts strategies are offered for inviting yourself personally and developing an imaginative orchestrating self. Realistic self-dialogue is presented as a way of dealing with the most intimate messages we send ourselves.

Chapters 5 and 6 explore establishing and maintaining inviting relationships. Chapter 5 looks at interpersonal leadership and what is involved in working with and for others. Developing an inviting stance and implementing the craft of inviting are offered as ways to establish and maintain doing-with relationships. Chapter 6 provides specific skills for managing conflict and dealing with philosophical differences. Examples are offered from front-line teachers and administrators to show how these skills can be put into practice.

The next pair of chapters explores the educational leader's relationship with values and knowledge. Chapter 7 looks at 'Leading for Values and Knowledge'. A self-concept-as-learner perspective is offered as the foundation of school programmes so that invitational leaders can work on constructing schools that care about mindful learning and disciplined understanding. Extending this to practical skills, Chapter 8 emphasises working from a caring core for invitational learning, the development of successful intelligence and the promotion of ethical fitness.

Chapters 9 and 10 deal with leading educational communities and managing them in productive ways. In Chapter 9, the conventional functions of schools are revisited from an inviting perspective. Using the metaphor of schools as inviting families rather than efficient factories, this chapter looks at the structure of inviting schools and the ways they call forth the educational development in all their members. Chapter 10 stresses that everything in schools matters and every way things are done matters. The 'five Ps' of invitational education (people, places, policies, programmes and processes) are highlighted and the invitational helix, a model for invitational change, is described.

Schools are not isolated compartments neatly detached from the larger society. Rather, schools and society are vitally connected in the project of constructing ethical and productive ways of living. The last two chapters in Part Two look at the inviting educational leader's relationship to the world outside the school. Chapter 11 looks at the role of the school leader as an advocate for educational living in a complex global society. Questions regarding ethical criteria for a more educational world are used to examine the inviting school's connection with the business world. The idea emphasised here is that leading for educational life needs to promote ecological responsibility, cognitive ingenuity and a deepening of democracy in everyday life. Chapter 12 is about taking the school out into the community, bringing the community into the school, and modelling democratic governance. The Inviting School Success Survey is offered as a way to do this.

The final part of the book is entitled 'Dare to Lead for Education'. It summarises the previous chapters and promotes the idea of leading for educational hopefulness. Chapter 13 'Sustaining Imaginative Acts of Hope', points out the persistence, resourcefulness and courage needed to speak and spread the language of inviting educational leadership.

This book is intended to be a living conversation about the nature of leadership, education and ethical ways to work. Each chapter in this book begins with an advance organiser about the topics covered and ends with questions and answers for extending the conversation. Chapters build on previous chapters. This is the way a theory of practice grows.

Inviting Educational Leadership is about more than surviving in the management jungle, although that certainly is important. Rather, it is about finding ways to savour, understand and better the experiences in the educational rainforest by using a communicative theory of care-based ethics. It is my hope that this book will encourage conversations about what is essential in education and how educators can work together in educational ways for educational purposes. It is my hope that these conversations lead to sustained imaginative acts of hope that will call forth a deepening commitment to educational life.

Part One

■ ■ ■

Inviting
Educational Life

1

■   ■   ■

Leading for Educational Life

Education is fundamentally an imaginative act of hope. Leading for educational life is about encouraging and sustaining the context in which imaginative acts of hope thrive.

What is education?

Why did you choose to become an educator?

What sustains you in your daily educational work?

How do you want to grow as a result of being an educator?

Because of the reflective commitment required to be a life-long educator, these are vital questions that need to be continually examined to keep educational beliefs alive. This book is *unlikely* to connect with your beliefs if you:

- think that education is limited to what goes on in schools;
- became an educator primarily because of the money;
- take daily delight in ordering others around;
- want to become a burned-out cynic;
- think this 'vision thing' is hopeless.

This book is more *likely* to connect with your beliefs if you:

- think education goes well beyond the schools;
- became an educator because you want to make a difference;
- enjoy working with people on meaningful projects;

- believe you can continually grow and participate in others' growth;
- are involved in education because of an evolving vision of people, ideas and adventures.

Visions matter, although they certainly can be trivialised. Created with integrity, visions can point us in a desirable direction, affect the way we feel about life's possibilities, and shape how we frame our daily actions. The vision informing this book is that education is fundamentally an imaginative act of hope and that educational leaders are people who systematically call forth and sustain those imaginative acts of hope. This hope is manifested in the vision of trying to make schools the most educationally inviting place in town by educational leaders who are trying to live exemplary educational lives. This is a book for people who believe it desirable to be hopeful about people, ideas and adventures through educational living. The book is based on realising this vision.

The title of this book, *Inviting Educational Leadership*, was chosen with this attention to vision, people, ideas and adventures in mind. The book is about leadership – it is about:

- constructing a shared, hopeful vision;
- articulating that vision to a variety of audiences;
- enrolling participants in extending that vision.

Such leadership is vitally needed in today's schools if we are to defend and progressively extend educational purposes.

To go further, this book is about a particular type of leadership – educational leadership – that provides the distinct vision that can move schools in ethically thoughtful ways. Ethical thoughtfulness refers to a sensitivity to issues of right or wrong, better or worse, or conflicts of competing values. Educational leadership is inherently an ethical activity because its vision and articulation, and process for enrolling others in that vision, seek to make an improvement in individual and collective learning experiences. If we are seeking to improve ourselves and others, if we are concerned with issues of better or worse, if we are trying to reconcile competing goods, then we cannot avoid dealing with ethical issues. The question is not whether or not educational leaders have to deal with ethical tensions. That they do is a given. The question is how well can educational leaders survive and grow as they deal with ethical issues. Ethical growth requires that educational leaders are ethically fit (Kidder, 1996). An ethically fit style of educational leadership can best use ideas from business or other forms of leadership if it is cognisant of the distinct qualities aimed for in educational ideals and school practice. An ethically fit style of educational leadership can do this because it is grounded in the unique set of intentions and principles inherent in educational experiences.

Educational leadership is an ethical practice dependent on a heightened commitment to the importance of educational ideals and the subtleties of school practice. As an ethical practice, it cannot be separated from the means necessary to bring about change. This book takes the perspective that educational leadership can best occur when it is invited through a doing-with process that sees participants as valuable, able and responsible partners. This inviting, doing-with process involves taking a proactive stance towards the messages that are extended in micro and macro educational environments. More fully elaborated in other texts (Purkey and Novak, 1996; Novak and Purkey, 2001), this inviting approach is embedded in a communicative theory of ethical practice for calling forth human potential (Purkey and Novak, 1999). The inviting approach claims that people are informed of their identity by the messages they receive, and reform their character by the messages they choose to extend. Used in classrooms and counselling, it is now being applied to educational leadership. (The basic concepts of the inviting approach will be spelled out in more detail in the next chapter.)

Putting the three words together in its title – *Inviting Educational Leadership* – this book is about reasons for, and ways to, creatively call forth and sustain an ethical stance for personal fulfilment and professional functioning by attending to the communicative process among people, schools and society. The dual nature of the title describes both the practices of inviting educational leaders and their goal of inviting educational leadership in all who are involved in educational work. This first chapter presents a fuller description of the characteristics of an educational perspective and shows how this perspective provides a systemic framework for leading in educational life.

The need for an educational perspective

> *To put it simply, there is no surer way to bring an end to schooling than for it to have no end.*
>
> (Postman, 1996: 4)

Perhaps Neil Postman overstates his case. Perhaps not. The uncontentious point is that educators need to give serious thought to where their schools should be heading if they are to direct them on an educationally defensible course. This is important now perhaps more than ever, because of mounting pressures being applied regarding the ends and means of schools.

Educators throughout the democratic world are being challenged to comply with mandates to operate their schools more like businesses. Words like 'customers', 'competition' and 'change' are routinely used to describe the new global and educational reality. Although not opposed to change per se, many educators reject the ferocity of the business models that are being thrust upon them. Many are suspicious. Many feel that the language and aims of business diminish the important work they have been doing and cut out the heart of their educational sensibilities. Many agree with the law of proximity: 'The more often we import ideas from afar, the less likely that over time they will make a difference' (Sergiovanni, 1996: xiv). To be able to respond in an educationally informed way to the onslaught of mandates to redirect schools in businesslike directions, and to direct this redirection in educationally sound ways, it is necessary to get a clearer framework for thinking about schools and education.

More than three decades ago, Neil Postman and Charles Weingartner (1973) pointed out an important difference between education and schooling: education can be looked at as a personal and social ideal while schools should be seen as social institutions. Education and schools can be imaginatively related, but they are not the same. So, just as love is not the same as marriage (but we should work to make it a part of marriage) and justice is not the same as the law (but we should work to make it a part of the law), education is not the same as schools (but we should work to make it a part of schools). If we do not make the ideal–institution distinction, we run into real-life difficulties, such as thinking that everything done in schools is educational or that ideals do not matter.

Ideals matter, but they function differently from institutions. Ideals serve as a moral compass that point us in a direction we think we should be heading. They involve our deepest aspirations and can be re-examined and rethought, at least implicitly, through our daily work in schools. Educational ideals point to concerns well beyond the school; they relate to valued work and meaningful projects; and they can enable people to realise more of their potential by calling forth creative challenges.

Institutions, on the other hand, are historically developed, socially located, complex organisations that are continually responding to political, economic and social pressures. Schools are such institutions.

However, in spite of the fact that schools are complex organisations that are influenced by their time and place and are under pressure to change (often in contradictory ways), they possess certain institutional essentials that define them as a school. Thus, all schools, to function as schools, need to structure time and activities; define intelligence, worthwhile knowledge and good behaviour; provide evaluation, supervision and role differentiation; and be accountable to the public and to the future (Postman and Weingartner, 1973: 16–27).

Educators will use a variety of conventions to handle the essential functions of their institution. For example, they may run the school year-round, use strong disciplinary boundaries for teaching, and define computer literacy as the most worthwhile intelligence. Other schools may run ten months per year, use an integrated curriculum, or define emotional intelligence as their key theme. Schools may be self-managed or not. Conventions may vary, but some conventions will have to be used.

The key questions about conventions deal with the ideals that inform them and the realities they need to handle. Conventions have to be educationally defensible and practicably workable or else problems of direction or implementation develop. Later in this book we will deal with developing educationally sound conventions for schools. The important points to realise here are that education as an ideal is different than schooling as an institution, and that schooling involves having to deal with institutional essentials through a choice of conventions. An important part of an educational leader's job is to recognise these distinctions and judiciously develop a shared vision, provide articulation, and enrol participants in the process of successfully orchestrating ideal–institutional integration.

Orchestrating ideals and conventions

Successful orchestration of educational ideals and the choice of school conventions cannot be overwhelming or underwhelming. It involves the gentle, but persistent, art of finding the right 'whelm level'. For example, in Example A in Figure 1.1 there is an overwhelming situation in which ideals are out of touch with institutional actualities. Ideals are separate from conventions, with ideals either thought of as overwhelming unattainables or as mere verbal wordplay about pie-in-the-sky wishes. In either case, conventions continue without being substantively informed by ideals. Ideals and conventions are

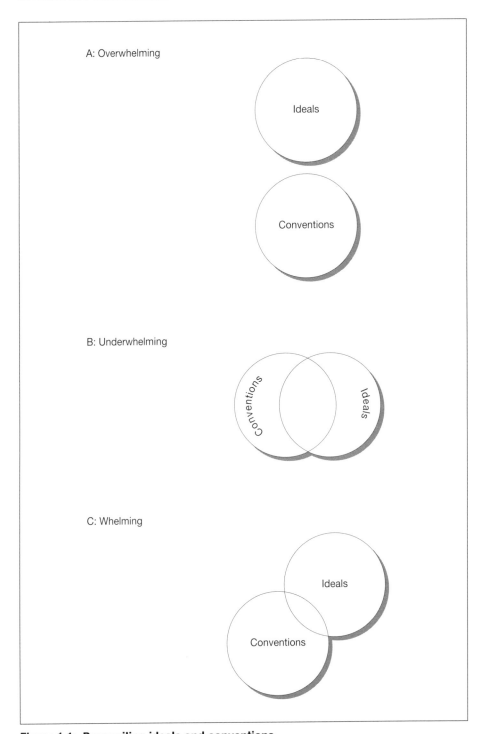

A: Overwhelming

Ideals

Conventions

B: Underwhelming

Conventions

Ideals

C: Whelming

Ideals

Conventions

Figure 1.1: Reconciling ideals and conventions

separate and separated. Example B, on the other hand, shows where the ideal and the conventions overlap considerably on the same level. In this case the ideals are underwhelming. They are seen, at best, as enthusiastic extenders of the status quo. Reaching ideals does not require much of a stretch – just keep doing what you have always been doing, but maybe, if you like, try a little harder. There is no extension of imaginative ethical thinking here, and people get locked into the idea that 'this is as good as it gets'. Interestingly, that statement can satisfy both the naïve optimist and the confirmed pessimist. Example C represents a 'whelming' situation where a healthy tension exists between ideals and conventions. Ideals connect with conventions and work to extend them. The ideal itself may not be realised, but, as Robert Nozick (1989) points out, ideals should not be judged on whether or not we attain them, but whether they take us further in a direction we consider worth heading. Ideals are deemed to be good to the degree that they actually provide movement in desirable directions. If an ideal does not do this, it has to be reconsidered. Active ideals are necessary for schools to remain purposeful and to improve.

One of the jobs of an educational leader is to see to it that people are not overwhelmed or underwhelmed, but to artfully structure the right whelm level for developing shared ideals. This works best within a context for educational living.

Educational living as an educational ideal

Without a narrative, life has no meaning. Without meaning, learning has no purpose. Without a purpose, schools are houses of detention, not attention.

(Postman, 1996: 7)

Perhaps again Neil Postman overstates his case. Perhaps not. His intention is to critique several current educational ideals and show how they lack the sense of purpose needed to encourage and sustain lasting, worthwhile school endeavours. Among the ideals he critiques are:

- *Economic utility*: you are what you do for a living. Schools are primarily for the purpose of training people for jobs.
- *Consumership*: you are what you accumulate. Schools are for the purpose of enabling people to have more possessions.
- *Technology*: you are an extension of the machine. Schools are to prepare people to fit into the technological society.

- *Tribalism*: you are only a member of a subculture. Schools are to teach people the superiority of their cultural group.

Postman's point is that each of these ideals is unable to furnish a shared narrative for an inspired reason for schooling. These ideals may supply short-term incentives for some, but not the deep-seated reasons needed to sustain the many in an endeavour as personally and socially important as schooling. Each of these ideals is short-sighted because it looks outside educational experience for an objective (or what Postman ambiguously calls an 'end') for schooling.

This book uses a person-centred approach for the purpose of inviting educational leadership. A person-centred approach takes as its starting point the importance of human experiences and the necessity to work within human experience to improve human experience. In other words, we can get more out of experience by getting more into it. Educational experiences are particular types of experiences that enable us to savour, understand and better more of our other experiences (Novak, 1997). They are worthwhile in and of themselves and enable us to grow. If we are able to develop and use the habits of savouring, understanding and bettering our experiences on a consistent basis, then we are living educationally. This, as John Dewey (1916) noted, is both the means and the ends of education.

Pursuing educational living can provide aesthetic, cognitive and moral direction, but not the details, for developing a shared educational ideal. It is a starting point for an educational conversation about a shared ideal. This shared ideal will have to be addressed again and again and refined in your particular context. Ideals, as was noted earlier, are not fully attainable ends but ethical means for living a more fulfilling life. Interestingly, as Dewey (1938) noted, the best way to learn to live educationally in the future is to try to live educationally in the present. The ideal of educational living, of seeking to savour, understand and better more of your experiences, is not something that educators can postpone.

The work of educational leaders is to construct the context in which the educative impulse to savour, enjoy and better more experiences can be orchestrated into a shared ideal that informs school practice. This is not easy, even in the most stable situations. It is even more complex in a pluralistic, postmodern world order that proclaims democratic aspirations, but questions universal standards. However, even in this postmodern age, where Anderson (1990) claims that 'reality isn't what it used to be' and the goal of arriving at a master narrative is suspect, most educators would agree that people are not realising educational ideals if, as a result of their schooling experiences, they are unable to:

- find ways to enjoy more of their daily experiences;
- work to understand more of the world, others and themselves;
- develop and implement strategies for improving individual and collective experiences.

The goal of educational living as a framework for educational ideals is to increase the educational quality of life not only for students, but for all involved in schools and beyond. Certainly, this can be overwhelming. However, if the job of educational leaders is not to overwhelm but to whelm, then leaders have to manage the delicate art of balancing appropriate celebrations of successes with raising dissonance about areas in need of improvement. This artful task is made easier with a systematic structure for focusing efforts.

A systematic structure for educational development

Educational growth is not the accumulation of more and more pieces of information, but the development of an increasingly complex structure for organising and interrelating ideas.

(Bannister and Fransella, 1980: 95)

Educational leadership, as described in this book, is different from other forms of leadership in two ways. First, it gets its impetus from the desirability of the educational ideal of educational living. Second, it can be uniquely focused on school practices. Educational leadership is about more than schools, but schools are a key institution for its realisation. The educational ideal described here is to have people lead more educational lives by learning how to savour, understand and better their individual and collective experiences. For this to happen, educators need to be students (attentive and systematic observers), teachers (wise and informed guides), leaders (persuasive and intelligent expanders), and managers (imaginative and persistent strategists) of educational living.

The goal of leading for educational living can be systematically approached by attending to the quality of the relationships that are embedded in the process of educational leading. Examined analytically, leading involves a person interacting with others so that something of value is accomplished.

This process takes place within an institutional arrangement and is intended to promote a certain type of social order. Figure 1.2 shows each of these components in the Educational LIVES model.

Beginning with the leader as a focal point, each of these components involves a relationship that can be used to give insight and direction for inviting educational leadership. For example, the *leader* (L) has a relationship with himself or herself that can be seen as summoning or shunning the personal potential necessary for leading an educational life. In addition, the leader has relationships with *individuals* (I) that can either call forth or negate a doing-with relationship necessary for shared involvement in an educational life. In addition, the leader has a relationship with *values and knowledge* (V) that either helps or hinders sound thought and wise action. Also, the leader has a relationship with an *educational community* (E) and its essential and conventional purposes. This relationship can support, neglect or subvert these purposes. Finally, the leader has a relationship with a larger *society* (S). The leader's relationship with this project can either be educative or miseducative. Inviting educational leadership is about savouring, understanding and bettering the quality of the five relationships of the Educational LIVES model.

Overview

Education lives through the educational lives of real people and their imaginative acts of hope. *Inviting Educational Leadership* is concerned with each of the five relationships in the Educational LIVES model of leading for educational life. It actively and ethically promotes relationships that call forth appreciation and potential in all who participate in schools so that educational living can be enjoyed and extended. Each of the relationships of the Educational LIVES model can be seen from an *inviting* perspective (focusing on the messages considered, intended, extended, received, interpreted and acted upon) and can also be examined from *leadership* (pointing to where we should be going) and *managerial* (showing us how we might get there) viewpoints. The combination of these perspectives provides the cumulative, systematic structure for this book. Chapters 3–12 focus on these five relationships in terms of leadership and management. The next chapter introduces the inviting perspective.

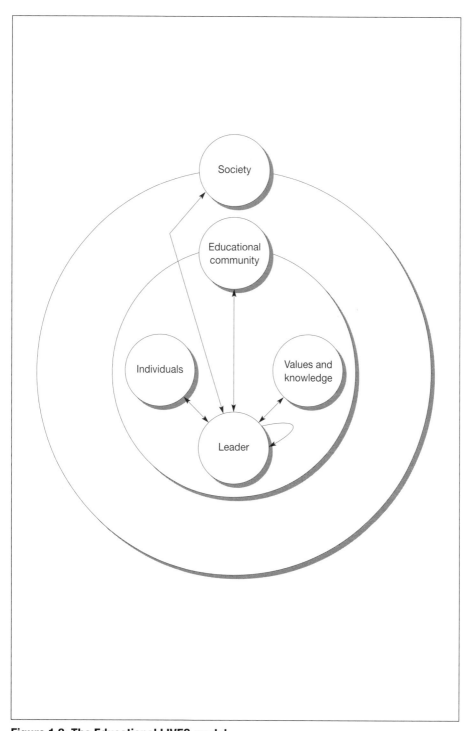

Figure 1.2: The Educational LIVES model

Summary

- The vision informing this book is that education is fundamentally an imaginative act of hope.
- Leadership is about visions, articulation and enrolling participants.
- Educational leadership is an ethical practice, which seeks to develop human potential.
- Inviting educational leadership focuses on the messages that call forth human potential.
- Education is an ideal and schools are institutions.
- Ideals have a better chance of making a difference if they do not overwhelm or underwhelm.
- Institutions have essentials and conventions.
- Institutional essentials can be met through a variety of conventions.
- Institutional conventions should be informed by ideals and also be workable.
- The ideal of living an educational life focuses on being able to savour, understand and better more individual and collective experiences.
- The Educational LIVES model emphasises the various relationships through which leaders can grow.

Extending the conversation

Q: Isn't it too idealistic to expect educators to be exemplars of educational living? That sounds like perfectionism.

A: Educators do not have to be perfect in living an educational life. That would be overwhelming. Rather, they have to believe in the *desirability* and *possibility* of leading an educational life and work thoughtfully to do this. Otherwise they run the risk of just going through the motions, and that's underwhelming.

Q: Isn't it just academic nit-picking to differentiate education from schooling?

A: Making distinctions can make an important difference in practice. Failure to distinguish between the realm of ideals and the institutional realms of essentials and conventions can lead to much practical confusion and much time wasted. Understanding that ideals serve the practical purpose of pointing us in a direction can allow us to focus our limited energy in the right places. So, sometimes there is nothing as practical as a good distinction.

Q: I have been 'visioned' to death when it comes to talking about leadership. Aren't we over this yet?

A: Perhaps the word 'vision' can be overused, but the concept is essential. If schools are not aiming to do something right, they are probably doing a lot of things wrong. More importantly, they will have no criteria for knowing what they are doing wrong. Visioning is just a way of finding out what we are saying 'Yes' to and then working out what we should do about it.

Q: The ideal of leading for educational living seems like mere wordplay. What is so important about leading for educational living and how is it different from business leadership?

A: Educational leadership should be different from business leadership in some essential ways because the essential purpose of education can be distinguished from the essential purpose of business. Business is primarily about making a profit. Education is about learning how to savour, understand and better more individual and collective experiences. Although you do not have to be rich to be a business leader or exemplary to be an educational leader, your credibility is enhanced if you are. In any event, people have the right to ask, 'If you think this thing called education is so important, why aren't you living it?'

Q: The Educational LIVES model seems very philosophical. That may be what you have to do at the academy but I work in the real world.

A: This book is not asking you to become an academic philosopher, but merely to distance yourself from some situations in order to see them steady and whole. The model offers a systematic way to look at the issues leaders face within themselves, with other people, with curriculum, with organisations and with society. Having a framework for looking at these issues can make them more manageable. That's a practical advantage.

Q: This book is too North American. We have our traditions you know.

A: The ideas in this book have been used with, and suggested by, educators throughout the world. They are not final thoughts but attempts to get new discussions going in ways that keep education alive in schools. Think of this book as an attempt to put an educational perspective on the agenda in discussions about globalisation.

Q: You keep talking about inviting this and inviting that. What is so special about this inviting approach?

A: I thought you would never ask. That's what the next chapter is all about. It's time to move on.

References

Anderson, W.T. (1990) *Reality Isn't What It Used To Be: Theatrical Politics, Ready-to-Wear Religion, Global Myths, Primitive Chic, and Other Wonders of the Postmodern World*. San Francisco: HarperCollins.

Bannister, D. and Fransella, F. (1980) *Inquiring Man: The Psychology of Personal Constructs*. 2nd edn. Malabar, FL: Kreiger.

Dewey, J. (1916) *Democracy and Education*. New York: Macmillan.

Dewey, J. (1938) *Experience and Education*. New York: Macmillan.

Kidder, R.M. (1996) *How Good People Make Tough Choices: Resolving the Dilemmas of Ethical Living*. New York: Fireside.

Novak, J.M. (1997) 'Doing Dewey right: pragmatic perspectives for politics and education', *Paidensis: The Journal of the Canadian Philosophy of Education Society* 10 (2), 13–24.

Novak, J.M. and Purkey, W.W. (2001) *Invitational Education*. Bloomington, IN: Phi Delta Kappa.

Nozick, R. (1989) *The Examined Life: Philosophical Meditations*. New York: Simon and Schuster.

Postman, N. (1996) *The End of Education: Refining the Value of School*. New York: Vintage.

Postman, N. and Weingartner, C. (1973) *The School Book*. New York: Delacorte Press.

Purkey, W.W. and Novak, J.M. (1996) *Inviting School Success: A Self-Concept Approach to Teaching, Learning, and Democratic Practice*. 3rd edn. Belmont, CA: Wadsworth.

Purkey, W.W. and Novak, J.M. (1999) 'An invitational approach to ethical practice in teaching', *The Educational Forum*, 63 (Fall), 37–43.

Sergiovanni, T.J. (1996) *Leadership for the Schoolhouse: How is it Different? How is it Important?* San Francisco: Jossey-Bass.

2

■ ■ ■

Invitational Leadership

The inviting approach seeks to connect with an educator's deepest intuitions, provide a logical foundation, and lead to ethical, productive and self-improving actions. Its focus is on the messages that are sent by people, places, policies, programmes and processes. Its aim is to make schools the most educationally inviting place in town.

What is essential in working with people?

Do the ends justify the means?

How important is it to take others' perceptions into consideration?

Do you think that all people matter?

Because of the personal commitment required to be a life-long educator, these are vital questions that need to be continually addressed to keep ethical practice alive. This chapter is *unlikely* to connect with your beliefs if you:

- would rather not work with people;
- believe that the ends justify the means;
- think that people are to be seen as objects to be conditioned;
- feel that only some people matter.

This chapter is more *likely* to connect with your beliefs if you:

- usually take delight in working with people;
- believe that ends and means are fundamentally connected;

- think that an individual's personal perspective is important;
- feel that all people matter.

Educational leaders are pushed and pulled from many, often conflicting, directions. Without a defensible framework for integrating their feelings, thoughts and actions, they run in many, often conflicting, directions. Without a defensible framework, their approach lacks educational integrity.

Educational integrity is about consistently operating from a perspective that brings together:

- *Feelings*: what you are doing should feel right and connect with and extend your deepest intuitions. (Educational leaders who cannot trust their deepest feeling are paralysed. If their deepest feelings are not examined, however, they run the risk of becoming dogmatic.)
- *Thoughts*: what you are doing should make sense and be capable of being articulated to a variety of groups. (Educational leaders who cannot speak to their deepest intuitions and actions from a clear, coherent perspective run the risk of becoming mere babblers or out-of-touch pedagogues.)
- *Actions*: what you are doing should lead to imaginative, self-correcting, ethical actions. (Educational leaders with deep feelings and sound thoughts who do not put these into consistent, self-correcting practice are not fully present and are merely going through the motions. They are leading a divided life and teaching others to do so.)

This chapter introduces invitational education as a theory of practice for leading with integrity.

The inviting approach

Inviting educational leadership is about working with people and ideals. More specifically, it is about realising the ideal of appreciating people in their uniqueness and finding imaginative and ethical ways to summon their potential to savour, understand and better more of their individual and social experiences. This ideal is facilitated by using a hopeful, action-based approach called invitational education that seeks to integrate an educator's feelings, thoughts and actions.

Invitational education is a system of assumptions, concepts and strategies for developing and sustaining imaginative acts of hope in schools and beyond. Based on the idea that education is an ethical activity in which human potential is called forth rather than dictated or manipulated, invitational education emphasises the quality of doing-with, dialogical relationships. By focusing on the messages that are sent and received, it is a communicative theory of ethical practice that aims to create educational contexts in which people want to be and learn.

As an evolving theory of ethical practice, invitational education is based on five interlocking assumptions (Purkey and Novak, 1996: 3):

1 People are able, valuable and responsible and should be treated accordingly.
2 Educating should be a collaborative and co-operative activity.
3 The process is the product in the making.
4 People possess untapped potential in all areas of worthwhile endeavour.
5 This potential can best be realised by places, policies, programmes and processes specifically designed to invite development and by people who are intentionally inviting with themselves and others personally and professionally.

These assumptions require elaboration.

To say that invitational education is an evolving theory of ethical practice means that it is a work in progress, incomplete and awaiting further development in research, theory and practice. Inviting educational leadership also means advancing the research, theory and practice of invitational education by trying out, evaluating and improving its key ideas. As a *theory* it is a way of thinking about something, in this case the development of human potential. This way of thinking has its unique set of assumptions and principles. (Later we will see the foundations and basic concepts of this theory.) As an *ethical practice* it involves a commitment to established co-operative activities, which contain unique standards of excellence that need to be conserved, examined and extended for more professional conduct to ensue. Practice, looked at this way, provides the impetus and criteria for evaluating and extending theory. The role of a theory of ethical practice is not only to make intelligence practical, but, more importantly, to make our practices more intelligible and more valuable. Putting this altogether, invitational education, as an *evolving theory of ethical practice*, is an emerging way of thinking about what it is that is worth doing well in developing human potential.

All theories make assumptions. Because invitational education is a theory of ethical practice it makes assumptions about what people are and how they should be treated. Assuming the ability, value and responsibility of all people (Assumption 1) commits educators to use ethical approaches that summon people to take ownership for their learning and behaviour. Seen this way, people are not objects to be shaped but persons worthy of appreciation and capable of self-growth.

The collaborative/co-operative nature of the educational process means that teaching, learning and leading (Assumption 2) are dialogical activities that involve doing-with rather than doing-to relationships. Dealing with people is ethically different from dealing with things, because people need to invest emotionally and morally in shared activity. Things, in contrast, can be seen as mere objects.

Relating the process to the product (Assumption 3) is a way of saying that what you do along the way affects what you end up with. The means are a part of the ends because human actions live on in the events that follow. Unethical means live on in the minds and reputations of those involved and those mindful of what has happened.

Recognition of the untapped potential of all people (Assumption 4) is a realisation that we are only a small part of what we can become intellectually, socially, physically, emotionally and morally. The possibility of connecting with the energies and interests of people through worthwhile possibilities that encourage appreciation, refinement and future growth is the basis for educational hope. Because we can become more than we presently are, there is always the possibility of growth.

The last assumption is based on the idea that just as everyone and everything in hospitals should encourage healing, everyone and everything in schools should serve educational purposes. The inviting educational leader's role is to participate in the orchestration of events that make this possible. This is done by focusing on the messages that are sent and received in schools and beyond.

The invitational approach

Leaders articulate and define what has previously remained implicit or unsaid; then they invent images, metaphors, and models that provide a focus for new attention.

(Bennis and Nanus, 1985: 39)

Invitational education is based on the metaphor that the educative process is comparable to the act of inviting, or calling forth, participation in activities that provide opportunities for savouring, understanding and bettering experiences. Inviting educational leadership is about encouraging, supporting and extending the quantity and quality of inviting messages.

An invitation can be defined as the summary of the content of messages communicated verbally, non-verbally, formally and informally through people, places, policies, programmes and processes. Inviting messages inform people that they are valuable, able and responsible and can behave accordingly.

Foundations of invitational education

Invitational education aims to provide an ethical and imaginative context for schooling. Just as a Christmas tree provides a context for decorative ornaments, invitational education provides a context for the various activities undertaken in the name of schooling. This integrative context needs solid foundations in order to be articulated with depth and sensitivity (*see* Figure 2.1).

Invitational education has three interlocking foundations:

1 *Democratic ethos*: a belief that all people matter and can meaningfully participate in their self-rule.
2 *Perceptual tradition*: a perspective emphasising that people need to be understood according to how things seem to them.
3 *Self-concept theory*: a viewpoint that all people are internally motivated to maintain, protect and enhance their perception of who they are and how they fit into the world.

Each of these three foundations requires further elaboration.

Democratic ethos

> *The moral development of a civilization is measured by the breadth of its sense of community.*
>
> (Anatol Rapoport, (cited in Homer-Dixon, 2000: 396)

Democracy, like education, is an ideal, an imaginative act of hope. This belief that everyone matters and can participate meaningfully in their self-rule is a recent development that is still being contested in many places.

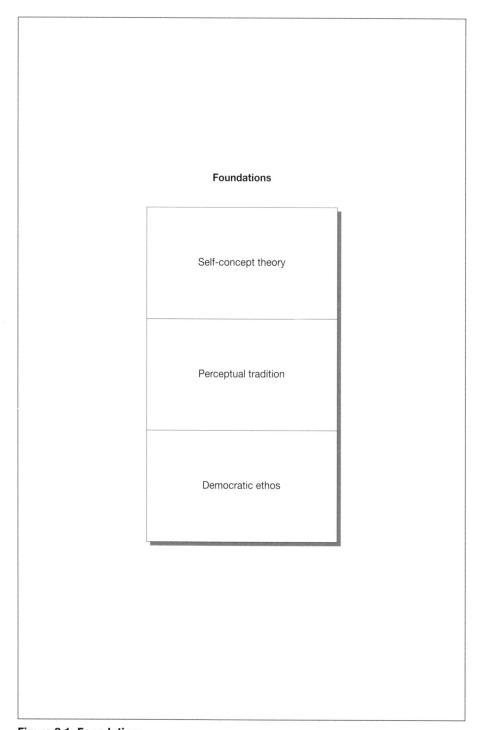

Figure 2.1: Foundations

At a minimum level, this belief in democracy can be justified (as Winston Churchill noted) by comparing democracy, with all its flaws, to its alternatives. On a more positive side, invitational education emphasises the democratic ethos because democracy can be viewed as the most educative social arrangement. By focusing on this doing with quality of social arrangements there is a commitment to the sense that 'we are all in this together'.

To say that all people matter is to say that it is not only the powerful, not only the attractive, not only the connected, not only the ones we are close to matter. An important part of this democratic ethos is not the vertical ascent to a final ethical truth (this seems unworkable in a pluralistic postmodern world) but rather a horizontal progression moving to include more and more people into the conversation of humanity, or, what Richard Rorty (1999) notes as a 'we intention'. This emotional, intellectual and practical understanding of humanity's fundamental connectedness requires an educative commitment to deliberative dialogue and inclusive respect, so that people can develop the character, practices and institutions that promote a more meaningful shared life. Seeking to realise the democratic ideal as an educational aim provides a direction and way of uniting people.

The perceptual tradition

Democracy emphasises the social nature of all people. The perceptual tradition looks at the 'ineliminatable' personal nature of each individual. Looking at the person from the inside out, the perceptual tradition postulates that there is no such thing as illogical behaviour. At the moment of behaviour, every person is doing what makes the most sense to him or her.

Taking the perceptual tradition to heart enables educational leaders to look at the meaningfulness of each person's actions from that person's point of view. In doing so, there is the potential to extend 'we intentions', to develop empathic relationships with even larger numbers of people. This also creates a practical vehicle for deliberative dialogue through shared understanding, because others are not viewed as foreign objects who behave in mysterious ways but as fellow humans seeking meaning.

Understanding the perceptual tradition also enables educational leaders to know that people usually operate according to the First Law of Ladder Climbing: do not let go of what you have a firm grasp of until you have a firmer grasp of something else. Ignoring this in attempting to get people to change is to encourage superficiality and restraint. Learning to understand an individual's behaviour from the inside out is a necessary step in developing empathy and meaningful change.

Self-concept theory

People's perceptions are their psychological realities. The most intimate perception people have is their self-concept – the belief they have about who they are and how they fit into the world. This most personal perception is maintained, protected and enhanced by every feeling, thought and action a person manifests.

The most tangible way a self-concept displays its workings is in a person's self-talk – the ongoing internal dialogue that goes on in all people. Teaching ourselves realistic and positive self-talk is an important step in living an educational life. (This will be examined in more detail in Chapter 4.)

Looking at each person from the inside out enables perceptualists to postulate that there is only one kind of motivation – the internal and continuous incentive to maintain, protect and enhance one's self-concept. Taking this perspective frees invitational educators from trying to motivate others. Seeing all people as continually motivated (if they were not motivated they would not be able to do anything, even resist) frees leaders to seek to connect with others to overcome obstacles and move in mutually positive directions. This requires sustained imaginative acts of hope and an awareness of categories of behaviour that fall short of this requirement.

Levels of inviting

As Abraham Maslow (1968) noted, we are never neutral in our interactions with others. Everything we do either calls forth or shuns human potential. Attention to the messages people send and their resolve in sending those messages provide a four-level classification system for examining what takes place in and around schools. This four-level classification system is an admitted simplification, but it can give an educational leader a language for discussing what is and should be happening in schools (*see* Figure 2.2).

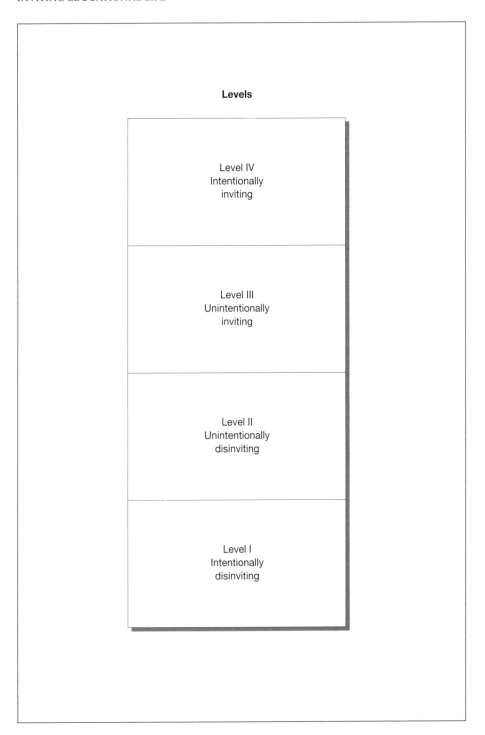

Levels

Level IV
Intentionally
inviting

Level III
Unintentionally
inviting

Level II
Unintentionally
disinviting

Level I
Intentionally
disinviting

Figure 2.2: Levels

As a starting point, any message can be categorised as:

- *Intentionally disinviting*: done on purpose to negate someone's worth.
- *Unintentionally disinviting*: done without resolve but still negating another.
- *Unintentionally inviting*: done without reflection but having positive effects.
- *Intentionally inviting*: done on purpose for purposes that can be defended.

Each of these four levels requires further elaboration.

Intentionally disinviting

Intentionally disinviting behaviour is meant to take the heart out of others by demeaning, diminishing or devaluing a person's sense of identity or potential. These types of actions, sometimes done with great subterfuge, inform people that they are incapable, worthless and irresponsible. These types of behaviours say, 'Why do you, and your type, even bother showing up?'.

A key part of an educational leader's job is to learn to understand, but not justify, intentionally disinviting behaviour. Working to understand it can provide possibilities for changing it. Justifying it may be even worse than doing it because it sets the stage for it to continue. Invitational leaders work to break this cycle of disinviting behaviour so that it does not become a part of a school's culture. Knowing about and working to prevent circumstances that perpetuate intentionally disinviting patterns of behaviour are essential parts of becoming an inviting school leader.

Unintentionally disinviting

As debilitating as intentionally disinviting behaviours can be, they are rare in comparison to unintentionally disinviting behaviour. These behaviours are not intended to harm but have that effect because an educator may be out of touch or insensitive to how his or her behaviour is being perceived. Unintentionally disinviting behaviour is manifested in unreflective ways of doing things and unimaginative school practices. Because things may not be working well, teachers tend to blame their students, and administrators blame their teachers. This epidemic of blame is seen in low teacher morale and students dropping out of school either physically or psychologically. The job of educational leaders is to be aware of such behaviours and suggest strategies to move in reflective, positive directions.

Unintentionally inviting

Educators at the unintentionally inviting level have found things that work and keep doing them over and over again. Often these likeable and good-natured individuals are successful, but when things change, they do not change too. Trying to do the same thing over and over again and facing difficulty often leads unintentionally inviting educators to regress to lower levels of functioning in which they blame others or seek revenge. Being out of touch sets the stage for giving up.

The job of educational leaders is to make explicit what is working and to provide an understanding of why it is working. Discussing previously unreflective school practices can be a way to introduce intentionality into the inviting process.

Intentionally inviting

Being intentionally inviting is to do things on purpose for purposes one can defend. It is to exhibit educational integrity to such a degree that one's feeling, thoughts and actions have a congruence. It is to focus on a sense of connectedness and creativity in informing people of their worth, value and responsibilities. This involves being able to learn from and grow through the tensions and setbacks that occur in attempting imaginatively to call forth human potential in often resistant and cynical settings. What is required here is what Patrick Slade (2001) calls the habits of hope – persistence, resourcefulness and courage. Although it can be demanding, inviting educational leaders seek to work with the habits of hope in all the areas of their lives. This means that they not only attend to the needs and concerns of others, but also to their own.

Areas of inviting

If the basic ideas of invitational education are good for other people, they should also be good for oneself. To be intentionally inviting on a consistent basis requires a deep sense of hopefulness. This sense of hopefulness is best nurtured when educators are inviting to themselves and others, both personally and professionally. It is through the orchestration of invitations in these four areas that invitational integrity develops. Each area requires enrichment and contributes to the integration of the personal and professional selves that educational leaders need if they are going to be involved in education for the long run. Each of the four areas will be looked at briefly and will be expanded on in later chapters (*see* Figure 2.3).

Inviting oneself personally

A key idea of the inviting approach is that all involved can find ways to enjoy the process. Because the inviting approach is person-centred, the individual doing the inviting needs to nurture his or her own personal development in order to deepen educational integrity. To be constantly living for others is to build up frustration and resentment, ironically, in both oneself and others. The personal commitment and imagination needed to call forth the potential in others is nurtured and modelled by being personally inviting with oneself. Finding ways to celebrate everyday life, recharge one's psychological batteries, and live life with a flourish is a necessary, but not a sufficient, task for invitational leaders.

Inviting others personally

Being intentionally inviting is about developing caring and trusting relationships with others. This means cultivating a solid support group – family, friends and colleagues with whom you can share important experiences. In schools, the development of an imaginative social committee can be important in keeping the celebratory spirit alive. With the development of online chat groups, this personal connection can be sustained with friends and colleagues across the globe. Finding ways to promote civility, to let people know you care and to break bread together are vital to supporting your support group.

Inviting oneself professionally

There is an old joke in education that says we have created great schools but they keep sending us the wrong kids. That may be what it feels like if educators do not keep up with the experiences of their children and the new developments in teaching and learning. Inviting oneself professionally means being involved in advanced degree programmes, doing action research, and reading, writing and conferring with colleagues. It is easy for educators to get into ruts.

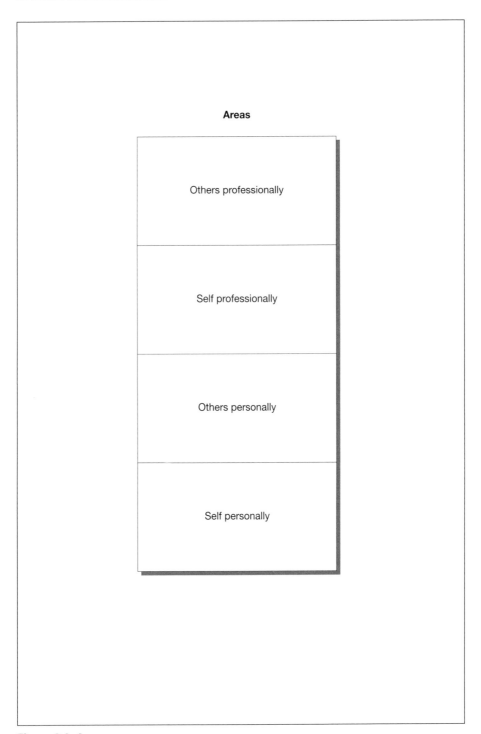

Areas

Others professionally

Self professionally

Others personally

Self personally

Figure 2.3: Areas

Many have been in schools most of their lives and have just gone from one side of the desk to the other when they became teachers. Finding new ways to do old and new things is essential to staying alive professionally. Joining professional groups and seeking feedback from colleagues, students, support staff and parents are ways to continue to grow professionally.

Inviting others professionally

The Educational LIVES model presented in Chapter 1 showed how it was important for leaders to use their personalities, relationships, knowledge, organizational experiences and social commitments to cordially and creatively summon human's potential. The next section of this book will explore leading ideas and management strategies for doing this systematically and imaginatively, building on the key concepts of invitational education. As important as it is to invite others professionally, it is not done in isolation from one's personal and professional lives. The artful orchestration of these four areas and the deepening understanding and use of the democratic ethos, the perceptual tradition, and self-concept theory enables inviting educational leaders to be in it for the long run.

Summary

- Educational leaders act with integrity when they integrate feelings, thoughts and actions.
- Invitational education is a system of assumptions, concepts and strategies for sustaining imaginative acts of hope in schools.
- Invitational leaders try to clarify their assumptions about people, education, ethics, possibilities and ways of proceeding.
- Invitational education is anchored in the democratic ethos, perceptual tradition and self-concept theory.
- Invitational leaders strive to eliminate intentionally disinviting behaviour and change unintentionally disinviting behaviour.
- Invitational leaders work to become intentionally inviting.
- In order to be involved in educational living in the long run it is necessary to invite oneself and others, personally and professionally.

Extending the conversation

Q: The word 'invite' does not seem tough enough to deal with the realities that today's educators face. Why did you chose this soft sounding word?

A: The word 'inviting' was chosen because it describes a more accurate representation of the teaching-learning-leading processes. We cannot force other people to learn meaningfully or follow enthusiastically. Their thoughtful effort is required. Focusing on imaginative and persistent ways to call forth their participation requires using a different metaphor. Leading as inviting was chosen because it more accurately attends to the choices and responsibilities involved in doing-with relationships. Although no one word can perfectly describe the teaching-learning-leading processes, it seems better to use a more accurate unusual word than an inaccurate familiar word. Sticking with the inaccurate familiar word does not seem strong enough to deal with the complexities that educators face.

Q: How does the inviting approach help people to lead with educational integrity?

A: If educators compartmentalise their feelings, thoughts and actions, they are at odds with themselves. Being in continual internal conflict closes off creative resources and speeds up burn-out. Developing an approach that integrates feelings, thoughts and actions in one's personal and professional life enables educators to focus, explore and grow. Our lives can be seen as creative works in progress rather than compartmentalised fortresses under siege.

Q: Practitioners need practical ideas. Why so many abstract ideas?

A: Educators are constantly being overwhelmed by the fad of the month. Without a solid grounding, they will be doing contradictory or unsubstantial things. In something as important as education, it is vital to have a sound and defensible way to think about things that are worth doing well. This is what an invitational theory of practice tries to do. Done well, it should lead to co-ordinated and substantial educational practices.

Q: People are always doing illogical things. What do you mean there is no such thing as illogical behaviour from the person's point of view?

A: From an external point of view behaviour may certainly seem illogical. People are always making mistakes and acting inconsistently on the evidence available from the outside. However, if we assume that from an internal point of view what is done at the moment of behaviour makes sense to the individual, we have the challenge to work out what must be going on in that person's lived world. This gets people to consider the other's intentions and circumstances and encourages the empathic imagination necessary to develop 'we intentions' essential for democratic living.

Q: Does using the perceptual tradition mean that we have to accept whatever a person does?

A: The perceptual tradition enables us to understand others better by trying to see that what they are doing makes sense to them at the moment of behaviour. However, because people do what makes sense to them does not absolve them of responsibility for their actions. Nevertheless, letting others understand that they are being understood is a start for developing inviting relationships.

Q: Does being intentionally inviting mean you have to be 'on' all the time?

A: The inviting approach has a perceptual orientation. This means that there is no particular behaviour that is inviting in itself. If being 'on' means being continually bubbly and enthusiastic, this can be very disinviting in some contexts. Too much of anything, even a good thing, can be too much. Variety of response and sensitivity to context are vital to the inviting approach. This develops best if we attend to how leaders relate to themselves.

Q: When will we be doing this?

A: Glad you asked. We are ready to move to this in the next two chapters.

References

Bennis, W. and Nanus, B. (1985) *Leaders: The Strategies for Taking Charge*. New York: Harper and Row.

Homer-Dixon, T. (2000) *The Ingenuity Gap*. New York: Alfred A. Knopf.

Maslow, A.H. (1968) *Toward a Psychology of Being*. New York: Van Nostrand Reinhold.

Purkey, W.W. and Novak, J.M. (1996) *Inviting School Success: A Self-Concept Approach to Teaching, Learning, and Democratic Practice*. 3rd edn. Belmont, CA: Wadsworth.

Rorty, R. (1999) *Philosophy and Social Hope*. London: Penguin.

Slade, P. (2001) *Habits of Hope: A Pragmatic Theory*. Nashville, TN: Vanderbilt University Press.

Part Two

■ ■ ■

Leading and Managing Educational Life

3
■ ■ ■

Personal Leadership

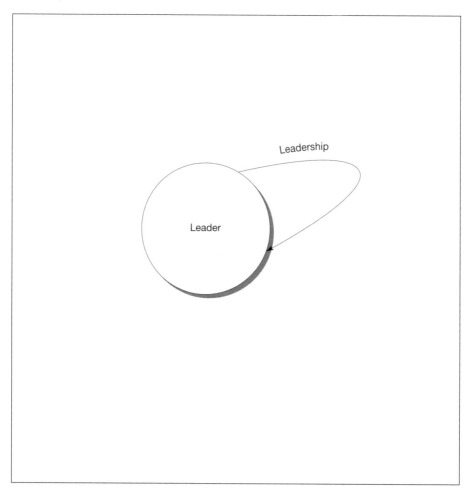

Figure 3.1: Personal leadership

Educational leaders need to live an educational life themselves if they are to call forth authentically this effort in others. This means being clear about what they are saying 'Yes' to in terms of the educational beliefs they espouse, being inclined to evolve a nuanced understanding of reality, perceptual processes and the self-concept.

What does it take to be in education for the long run?

What are you saying 'Yes' to in your educational life?

Do you think life can be neatly compartmentalised?

Is it important to be authentic in your personal and professional life?

Because of the authenticity needed to be a life-long educator, these are vital questions that need to be asked to keep educational beliefs alive. This chapter is *unlikely* to connect with your beliefs if you:

- think life can be neatly compartmentalised;
- think living a meaningful life is beyond your control;
- think being an educator means having to 'play the game';
- want to get out of education as soon as you can.

This chapter is more *likely* to connect with your beliefs if you:

- believe that your personal and professional life can be creatively integrated;
- view living a meaningful life as a creative challenge;
- believe that educational leaders can persistently act with integrity;
- are in education for the long run.

The educational philosopher John Dewey once said that educators must first of all be human, and only after that professional. This chapter explores issues that can provide guidance for personally inviting educational leadership. It examines the importance of personal beliefs and the necessity to find meaningfulness in the activities of everyday life.

Inviting educational leadership is too complex to be consistently faked. It eventually catches up with you if you are merely pretending to behave in an inviting manner. Like trying to hold a beach ball underwater, your true beliefs will come to the surface and you will have expended a lot of wasted energy. As a personal ideal, inviting educational leadership has to be lived intentionally, that is with a sense of authenticity, purpose and self-correcting persistence.

For example, Warren Bennis (1989) points out that leaders possess four key characteristics:

- *Positive other regard*: taking a concern for the well-being of others; finding delight in their successes and providing personal and material resources for them to be successful.
- *Balancing of ambition, values and competence*: orchestrating these three traits so as to avoid becoming a demagogue, ideologue or technocrat.
- *Wallenda effect*: not thinking about failing but thinking about what is necessary to succeed.
- *Emerson effect*: finding a spark in the stuff of everyday life.

In addition, Howard Gardner (1995), in his study of the qualities of leaders, found that leaders routinely demonstrated the confidence to speak to authority. They are not in awe of, or disrespectful to, those in authority, but feel capable of dealing with those in power in a thoughtful manner.

Now imagine trying to fake these characteristics on a consistent basis. Pretending to have a sense of other regard, balance, success and joy, and trying to consistently address those in authority with a false confidence would soon become disastrous. To paraphrase an old saying: you may be able to fool some of the people all the time, and all the people some of the time, but if you try to fool all the people all the time, you will just be fooling yourself, and looking foolish doing so. Your behaviour would lack character: commitment, complexity and credibility (Bennis and Nanus, 1997).

Rather than trying to learn behaviours to fit each of these leadership traits, inviting educational leadership works with what underlies all behaviours – perceptions or personal beliefs. The perceptual tradition stresses that people behave according to how they view self, situation and purpose (Combs, Miser and Whitaker, 1999). According to this perspective, person-centred educational leaders possess the following affirmative beliefs about self, situations and purpose:

- *Self*: a sense of efficacy; a feeling that one can make a difference.
- *Situation*: a sense of hopefulness; an energetic openness to positive possibilities.
- *Purpose*: a sense of educational ends; a feeling for the means to savour, understand and better more of the experiences one has.

Perceptions, as Combs described them in an earlier work (1982), are personal beliefs that make a difference. The beliefs required to be an intentionally inviting educational leader are not mere verbal statements one can easily assent to, but deep-seated dispositions to act with intentions in mind. Pursuing this deep-seated intentional way of functioning is not something done once and for all. Rather, it is a part of the development of an educational character, the ongoing process of being and becoming a leader for educational life. It is something every educator can work to clarify, refine and extend.

Inviting educational leadership requires educators to develop and use their personalities for educational purposes. It is heavily person-centred and requires educators who can operate from a perceptual viewpoint with trustworthy beliefs and a healthy sense of self. This is more likely to occur if educators possess a nuanced understanding of reality, perceptions and self.

Coming to grips with reality

Reality isn't what it used to be.

(Anderson, 1990)

In order for perceptualists to avoid solipsism – the belief that reality is merely what is inside your head – it is important to stress the facticity of external happenings: that there are events going on outside of us, and that there were events going on well before we arrived, and will continue well after we are gone. To paraphrase the portrayal by Berger and Luckmann (1966) of the social construction of reality: reality goes on within and without us. In other words, there is more that is going on than what we presently perceive, and our existence depends on our connections with the world outside our heads. If it did not, then, as my daughter pointed out to me several years ago, we would never have to go anywhere, move our bodies, or eat.

To understand personal beliefs associated with reality, it might help to think of a thought experiment developed by Robert Nozick (1989) that I have tried with educators throughout the world. Imagine you could take a pill that would put you in a blissful coma for the next 80 years. After that you would die. In this coma you would be perfectly happy and would not even know you took the pill. Nozick's question is this: 'Would you take the pill?' Although many people might be tempted to take the pill (the value of escape as a coping mechanism is not to be denied), I have found that most people say they would not take the pill because they want to seek happiness *within* reality. A mere delusional sense of pleasure would put them out of touch with what is really going on.

Our ethical sensibility as educators is that people should strive to live wide-awake, even while we acknowledge the tempting quality of escape. As educators we want to connect more deeply with this reality and its possibilities and surprises. The creative pursuit of more reality and the pursuit of creative and harmonious relationships within it are the grounds for savouring, understanding and bettering more of our experiences. To try to escape permanently or deny reality is to give up, to admit defeat. In this defeatist stance, consciousness becomes that annoying time between naps, and life something that is lived, at best, in small doses.

The development of educational character involves a commitment to seek meaning within reality. The meaning sought within reality is not something attained once and for all, but involves what Mihaly Csikszentmihalyi (1993) calls the evolving self seeking complexity. According to this point of view, people develop complexity as they are able to make more differentiations within reality that they then are able to put together in a more integrated fashion. In other words, people develop complexity when they perceive more than they previously perceived and construct more integrative frameworks for making sense of their expanding perceptions. Developing complex perceptions, from this point of view, is not, as Henry Ford said about history, 'one damn thing after another', but rather a series of flights and perchings that give us a deeper, more meaningful understanding of events and possibilities, along with a more credible life perspective. This life perspective is one that enables a person to become self-directed and 'to live in fullness, without waste of time and potential, expressing one's uniqueness, yet participating intimately in the complexity of the cosmos' (Csikszentmihalyi, 1997: 2). This is not the perspective of the escapist or defeatist.

Perceptions about perceptions

The development of an educational character involves a commitment to live life more fully by seeking to appreciate the reality around us and to develop more complex relationships within that reality. In addition, it requires a nuanced understanding of the subtleties of the psychological workings of the perceptual processes.

From the perceptual approach, people behave according to how the world seems to them, that is in conformity with the beliefs they possess and the differentiations they are able to make at the moment of behaviour. While we may want to achieve happiness within reality, we do not have immaculate perceptions. Our understanding of reality is always mediated by our perceptual processes. An understanding of some of these processes can enable us to work with, rather than against, them. There are eight basic points about the workings of our perceptual processes.

- *We can perceive things that can exist at one level but not another*. For example, a plan can seem like a good idea in the abstract but will not work in the concrete. So it is important to see in what ways a plan corresponds to what it is intended to bring about, and to modify it accordingly. This is why it has been said that an idea needs to be born in our head and then in our practice.

- *Logic is not the same as psychologic*. How people perceive something is not necessarily the same as how it can be shown to be. Rules of inference have their place, but if they do not connect with the personal differentiations individuals make in their lived-world, logic may be misplaced.

- *The focus of perceptions is affected by desires*. Often we look for what we want and need to see. If we did not, we would be bombarded by an infinite number of perceptions and have great difficulties attending to ourselves. However, desiring to perceive something and actually perceiving it are not the same thing.

- *Things can look different from different perspectives*. There are many different ways to look at an event. To think there is only one way is to be locked into what is called a 'hardening of the categories'. Being able to see things from many vantage points is a vital asset in a pluralistic world.

- *There is a tendency to lock into initial perceptions*. The habitual ways we are used to seeing things is the way we expect usually to see them again. If everything were totally different, then there would be perceptual chaos. Nothing would be coherent. However, when things change we often stick to our previous perceptions unless we are made aware that these perceptions are not working.

- *The past is used to anticipate the future*. Although we exist in the present, we use our memories of what has happened to prepare us for what might happen. The ability to imaginatively connect future goals with previous memories can provide previously unimagined possibilities.

- *Dissonance can be an invitation to growth if it is not overwhelming*. When we experience that a perception is inadequate we can choose to ignore it or explore it. Exploring a perceptual dissonance is a way to develop more complex perceptions. This is more likely to occur if the dissonance is interesting and the expected gain of the new perception can be seen to outweigh the modification of the old perception.

- *Perceptions are influenced not only by what is there but also by what is not there.* What is missing can be as, or more, important that what is present. What is unsaid in many situations can say more than what is said. Because we have expectations of what should be happening, we can notice what is missing.

Attending to these eight generalisations regarding the perceptual world enables educators to go beyond words, to attend to the psycho-logic, to look at things from a variety of perspectives, to work to go beyond initial impressions, to use memories, anticipations and desires in creative ways, to view dissonance as a possibility for growth, and to see what may be missing in any situation. Applying these understandings to the workings of their own self-concepts gives invitational leaders personal credibility in their character development.

Perceptions of self

If I am not for myself, who is for me?

(Hillel)

A nuanced understanding of perceptual processes enables invitational leaders to develop more complex relationships with others, the world and themselves. This latter relationship is vital to a leader's sense of well-being and his or her ability to lead for educational life.

There are various ways to portray the self system. William Purkey's spiral diagram provides a useful beginning (*see* Figure 3.2). According to this diagram, the global self system has three components: the 'I', or self-as-subject; the 'mes', or self-as-object; and the evaluations placed upon the 'mes', or self-esteem. Each of the components is a part of an organised whole.

The 'I' represents consciousness or awareness. It is the unique life-connection each person possesses. The idea that each person possesses a lived world, a world of internal meanings, is one way to separate people from robots. Without the perception that there are other 'Is' in the world, humans would feel few ethical constraints to objectifying others and using them for only instrumental purposes. The cry of the

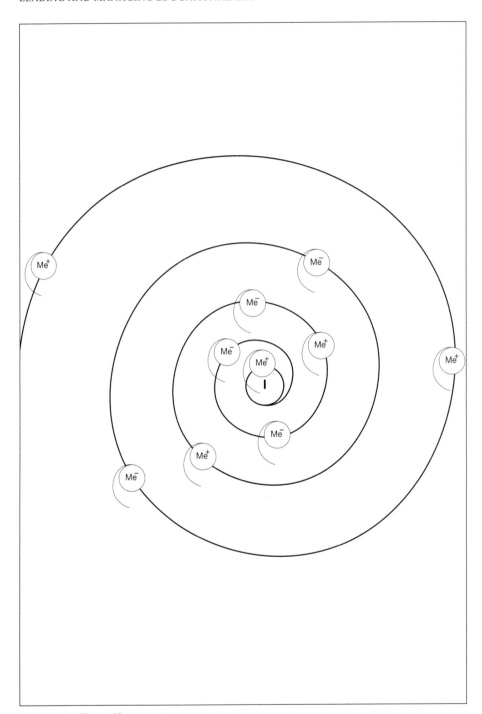

Figure 3.2: The self-concept
(*Source*: Purkey, 1970)

Elephant Man – 'I am a human being!' – represents a reaction to having one's sense of 'I-ness' – one's personhood – negated. Inviting educational leadership respects the 'I-ness' of everyone by viewing oneself and others as valuable, able and responsible.

The various 'mes' around the 'I' represent attributes and categories one sees oneself possessing. Attributes stand for characteristics such as joyful, serious, knowledgeable, ignorant, able or unable. Categories are exemplified in such words as male, female, English, Canadian, head-teacher or non-educator. The closer a 'me' is to the centre of self, the more it influences awareness. Although peripheral 'mes' are only attended to infrequently, over time there can be movement, enrichment and replacement of the 'mes'.

Just as we are not neutral to our own existence, the 'I' is not neutral in its evaluation of the 'mes'. Each 'me' is evaluated in positive or negative terms. This evaluation may be fair or unfair, but it is real to the person making the evaluation (Purkey, 2000). People with positive evaluations of 'mes' close to the 'I' are seen to possess positive self-esteem. Those with negative evaluations are seen to possess negative self-esteem. For example, if I view myself as an athlete, and by objective criteria I am a very good athlete, but I am always comparing myself to world-class performers, I may feel negative about myself in this category. The logical is not necessarily the psychological.

An important part leading for educational life is to be aware of the operation of one's self-system: how the 'I' becomes clear or unclear about various 'mes'; the closeness of various 'mes' to the centre of self; the change in 'mes' over the years; the projected 'mes' one anticipates; the struggle to move new 'mes' in and out of the centre; the way in which one listens to the 'mes' as one makes decisions in daily life. Understanding the working of the self is a complex and fascinating endeavour.

Just as a healthy body does not guarantee that someone will not get hurt or sick, so too a healthy self-system does not guarantee that someone will be able to handle all life's hardships. Reality does not seem to have human needs in mind. It can throw some serious obstacles at people. A healthy self-system does, however, give a person a better chance to recover and learn from the obstacles, which at times may seem overwhelming.

Making the overwhelming creatively whelming is an important characteristic of personally leading for educational life. For example, Howard Gardner (1995) has shown that leaders who possess a healthy sense of self demonstrate three abilities:

- *Reflecting*: to be able to step back and see the point of an activity and understand implications for the future.
- *Leveraging*: to be able to capitalise on their strengths and take something they can do well and apply it within a leadership situation.
- *Framing*: to be able to learn from unsuccessful experiences and use these learnings to generate new ways to deal with current issues.

Each of these three abilities can be seen to be parts of an orchestrating educational self, a self that seeks artfully to lead a meaningful life. This orchestrating self works with a nuanced understanding of perceptual processes as it tries to bring the various 'mes' into a fulfilling and harmonious relationship with an evolving reality.

The centre of the educationally orchestrating self is the 'I' (the awareness of the present). This awareness of the present can be seen in degrees of receptivity or unreceptivity to the ongoing stream of events. In dealing with issues, the educationally orchestrating self views them in terms of maintaining, protecting and enhancing the self-concept. By creatively using the past to anticipate a variety of futures and developing habits of persistence, resourcefulness and courage, the orchestrating self is able to transform desires into imaginative desirables. This is the process of pursuing imaginative acts of hope in one's personal life. Some strategies for doing this will be presented in the next chapter.

Summary

- Inviting educational leadership is not something that can be consistently faked.
- The perceptual tradition emphasises beliefs about self, situations and purposes.
- Perceptions need to be connected with possibilities in reality to avoid becoming escapist or defeatist.
- Educational leaders can learn to work with rather than against their perceptual processes.
- The self-system includes the 'I', 'me' and assessment of life possibilities.
- Everyone is continually motivated to maintain, protect and enhance his or her self-system.
- Invitational leaders work to develop an educationally orchestrating self.

Extending the conversation

Q: This chapter stressed the importance of having authentic beliefs. How do you know if you authentically believe something?

A: Authentic beliefs are intimately connected with feelings and practices. If a belief is authentic then a person should be consistently living by it in his or her daily existence. That would mean that living by this belief would make a person feel honest. Acting in opposition to it would make a person feel hypocritical. Not attending to it would make a person feel empty.

Q: What is it that inviting educational leaders are saying 'Yes' to?

A: In terms of this chapter, inviting educational leaders are saying 'Yes' to living fulfilling lives by developing authentic, deepening connections to reality, others and themselves. Chapters 5, 7, 9 and 11 will explore what they are saying 'Yes' to in terms of relationships, knowing, working and democratic practice.

Q: Don't you have to fake it sometimes? Isn't it better to fake interest than be rude? Wouldn't being rude hurt another's self-concept?

A: Invitational leaders may not have their whole heart, mind and will into everything they do but they can work at being open to this possibility. There are various reasons to be interested in what is happening.

49

Invitational leaders try to tune into at least one of these reasons and often find other reasons in the process. They do not want to make a habit of faking interest.

Q: How do people obtain the perceptions of person-centred educational leaders?

A: You can try on these perceptions and act as if you were operating from this framework. By seeing how the world would be different if you worked from a person-centred perspective you can begin to examine your present perceptions. Reflecting on the differences can be an invitation to keep, modify or extend your present beliefs.

Q: Doesn't each person have his or her own reality? Are you saying you know what reality is for each person?

A: Although each person has a psychological world that needs to be considered, some things go on whether we are aware of them or not. Being aware of the possibility of perceptions beyond our present perceptions is a way to be open to growth.

Q: If more people said that they would be willing to take Nozick's sleeping pill, does that make taking the pill the right thing to do?

A: If more people are willing to take the pill, this tells us something about the nature of the world in which we are presently dwelling. What is it about our present reality that would make people want to be permanently disconnected from others? As many parents used to tell their children, 'Just because everybody is doing it, doesn't mean it is a good thing to do'.

Q: Aren't we trying to make life simpler rather than more complex?

A: Simplicity enables us to put non-essentials aside and get to what is really important. This can be very important for living an uncluttered life. The pursuit of complexity is not the pursuit of clutter but a commitment to the belief that we can experience life more deeply and broadly.

Q: If logic is not the same as psychologic, does this mean that we are all illogical?

A: We may appear illogical from an outsider's perspective but we tend to act consistently in terms of how things seem from our insider's perspective. Psychologic is about the logic or consistency of this insider's perspective. If there were not an internal logic, all behaviour would be capricious. Sometimes, however, it takes time to uncover this internal logic.

Q: Dissonance does not feel good. Shouldn't it be avoided?

A: Dissonance may not feel good, but it does not have to feel bad. It can be used to show us that we are not infallible, something we know on one level but may not have accepted on other levels. Learning to cultivate dissonance can be a way of growing. Interestingly, the scientific method works this way and I do not think it should be avoided.

Q: Does your self-concept make you do something?

A: Your self-concept is not the cause of behaviour; it is not something we can blame for what we do. Rather, the self-concept can be seen as a connected system of beliefs from which we habitually act. These beliefs can be examined and modified to serve educational purposes, thus enabling a person to have a deeper sense of autonomy and purpose.

Q: It sounds like the educationally orchestrating self is doing a continual juggling act. Isn't anything stable?

A: Similar to flying in a plane, although everything is moving, some things are more stable and tied down than others. These more stable elements are used to steer the plane. For the orchestrating self, key values, beliefs and habits provide the direction. These, however, can be examined if the direction in which one is heading seems undesirable.

Q: How do you put these ideas into practice?

A: I thought you would never ask. It is time to deal with some practicalities in the next chapter.

References

Anderson, W.T. (1990) *Reality Isn't What It Used To Be: Theatrical Politics, Ready-to-Wear Religion, Global Myths, Primitive Chic, and Other Wonders of the Postmodern World*. San Francisco: HarperCollins.

Bennis, W. (1989) *The Leadership Challenge: Skills for Taking Charge*. New York: Macmillan. (Audiotape.)

Bennis, W. and Nanus, B. (1997) *Leaders: The Strategies for Taking Charge*. New York: Harper and Row.

Berger, P. and Luckman, T. (1966) *The Social Construction of Reality: A Treatise in the Sociology of Knowledge*. Garden City, NY: Doubleday.

Combs, A.W. (1982) *A Personal Approach to Teaching: Beliefs that Make a Difference*. Boston: Allyn and Bacon.

Combs, A.W., Miser, A.B. and Whitaker, K.S. (1999) *On Becoming a School Leader: A Person-Centered Challenge*. Alexandria, VA: Association for Supervision and Curriculum Development.

Csikszentmihalyi, M. (1993) *The Evolving Self: A Psychology for the Third Millennium*. New York: HarperCollins.

Csikszentmihalyi, M. (1997) *Finding Flow: The Psychology of Engagement with Everyday Life*. New York: HarperCollins.

Gardner, H. (1995) *Leading Minds: An Anatomy of Leadership*. New York: BasicBooks.

Nozick, R. (1989) *The Examined Life: Philosophical Meditations*. New York: Simon and Schuster.

Purkey, W.W. (1970) *Self-Concept and School Achievement*. Englewood Cliffs, NJ: Prentice Hall.

Purkey, W.W. (2000) *What Students Say to Themselves: Internal Dialogue and School Success*. Thousand Oaks, CA: Corwin Press.

4
■ ■ ■

Managing an Educational Life

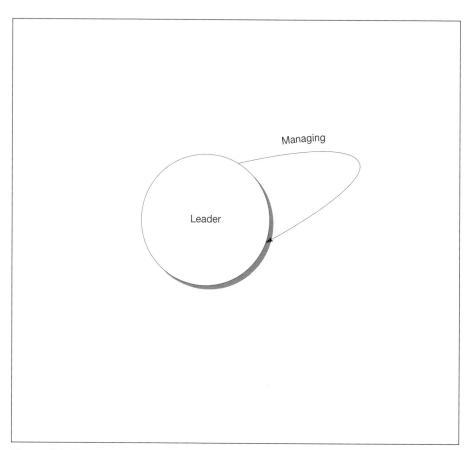

Figure 4.1: The managing self

Managing a fulfilling life requires developing an orchestrating self that is able to savour, understand and enjoy more of life's daily experiences. This is done by personally inviting active elements of enjoyment, realistic and positive self-dialogue, and educational wellness.

What is involved in being able to enjoy an activity?

How do you address yourself when you make a mistake?

How do you put into practice basic principles of life management?

To what extent do you 'walk the talk' of putting your ideas into practice?

Because of the persistence required for being a life-long educator, these are vital questions needed to be asked in order to keep educational living alive. This chapter is *unlikely* to connect with your beliefs if you:

- think that you have no choice in most things;
- believe what you say to yourself is unimportant;
- consistently ignore your personal well-being;
- feel that there are unresolvable gaps between what you say and what you do.

This chapter is more *likely* to connect with your beliefs if you:

- think that you have many choices in most things;
- think that realistic and positive self-talk is within your control;
- try to find imaginative ways to invite yourself personally;
- work to use the tension between ideals and practices to improve both.

John Paul Sartre once said that we are condemned to be free. By that he meant that we always have choices. Even to refrain from making a choice is to make a choice. Not to acknowledge responsibility in making choices is to act in bad faith. This chapter is about managing choices with imaginative acts of hope in mind. It is about putting into practice some key ideas for inviting oneself personally.

The idea that 'the road to hell is paved with good intentions' reminds us that there is often a gap between what we think we should do and what we actually do. This is especially true in realising personal educational goals. As Shakespeare's Portia noted, 'I can easier teach twenty what were good to be done, than to be one of the twenty to follow my own teaching' (*The Merchant of Venice*, I,ii). Personally realising an educational life requires imaginative and persistent management strategies. Although there is no formula, there are some insights and strategies that can help in conducting an educationally fulfilling life. These strategies can enable us to savour, understand and better more of our daily experiences.

The use of life-management strategies can follow some basic principles of development noted by Jane Jacobs (2001). She noted that development can be viewed in terms of three basic principles:

- differentiation emerges from generality;
- differentiations become generalities from which further differentiations emerge;
- development depends on co-development.

Applying these principles to managing an educational life means that we can start with some basic insights and strategies that can be refined in practice, further refined in more refined thought and practice, and then brought in harmony with developing complementary practices. The strategies given will be generalities that will need to be developed in personal practice and then harmonised with other developing life habits. Since personal management is about leading an educational life, it is important to turn to strategies for savouring, understanding and bettering one's daily experiences.

Savouring daily experiences

There is an educational adage that states that experience is not what happens to you, it is what you do with what happens to you. This is partly correct. Certainly, an experience becomes educational if you do something useful with it. However, what you do while you are having an experience also enables you to do more with it later.

Mihayli Csikszentmihalyi has studied the psychology of optimal experience. In the 1990s he wrote three important books on the subject: *Flow* (1990), *The Evolving Self* (1993) and *Finding Flow* (1997). Each of these books deals with the development of a more complex self through challenging engagement with everyday life. If one of the goals of living education is to savour more of everyday life, then Csikszentmihalyi's practical method for finding flow can be beneficial. Fulfilling engagement with everyday life requires focus, persistence and modification so that 'the heart, will, and mind are on the same page' (1997: 28). Such challenging engagement is comprised of the following seven elements (1990: 48–67).

- *A challenging activity that requires skill.* This involves putting ourselves in situations where we are neither overwhelmed or underwhelmed. If we find ourselves overwhelmed, we can break a task into smaller steps and develop new skills. If we are underwhelmed, we can seek out ways to extend the tasks we have to face.

- *The merging of action and awareness.* This involves putting full attention to the task at hand. Our perceptual processes are focused and we become at one with what we are doing.

- *Clear goals and feedback.* Goals enable us to focus our attention. Feedback enables us to make the necessary adjustments. Without goals our activities are aimless. Without adjusting to feedback, our behaviour is mechanical.

- *Concentration on the task at hand.* Clearly and creatively structured tasks impose order on the perceptual processes. This imposed order prevents the disorder caused by ambivalent distractions.

- *The paradox of control.* As we are fully engaged in a task we are not worried about being out of control and simultaneously gain a deeper sense of connection and control.

- *The loss of self-consciousness.* Through an investment of attention in a challenging activity a person is not protecting a previous image of the self. Energy is not wasted holding previous images in mind.

- *The transformation of time.* We are not bound by the clock but respond to the inner pace of the activity.

Being able to construct flow activities in daily life is a part of becoming a self-directed learner, someone who can focus attention and extend learning through finding challenging activities in all he or she does. This habit involves negotiating the delicate balance between anxiety and boredom through tasks that have intrinsic meaning. It takes effort and practice, but when it is done well our worlds of work and play merge. This seeking flow in everyday life is an educational ideal that can focus and deepen our daily practices.

When this seeking of flow is connected with our sense of self, it can take on deep personal meanings. For example, the different 'mes' of our self, the various attributes we possess and categories we perceive we belong to, each have their own challenges and rewards. Working to orchestrate each of these 'mes' in terms of potential flow activities can provide an abundant and meaningful source for enjoyment and growth. This enables us to become creative directors of our lives, as opposed to being lived by external events or a rigid sense of self. Attention to internal events takes us further down this line.

Attending to the inner conversations of our life

Socrates pointed out the importance of knowing thyself. That is all well and good, but where are we to begin? If we think in term of seeking flow activities in daily life, then we can see how our current self is transcended. As important as transcendence is, it builds on the voices of our current sense of self.

The inviting approach is a communicative theory of human practice. One of the most intimate human practices we each have is the way we talk with ourselves. This inner voice is what William Purkey (2000) calls 'the whispering self'. This whispering self is the current self with a voice (p. 4). It is with us in our actions and reflections, and in particular in our judgements about who we are and how we fit in the world. How we orchestrate this inner speech influences the quality of our daily experiences.

Being intentional means doing things on purpose for purposes we can defend. This intentionality can be directed to our inner speech, especially when it is unrealistic and unnecessarily harsh. For example, often we will say things to ourselves about ourselves that we would not say to our worst enemy. Why? Because we think that nobody is listening? Because we think it is not important?

If our sense of self is informed by the messages we receive and formed by the messages we construct, the importance of realistic and positive self-talk becomes obvious. What has happen to many of us is that often we have come to use unrealistic, inappropriate or unduly harsh talk with ourselves. For example, several years ago I was playing tennis with a friend and every time he missed a shot he would berate himself. I stopped the game and went to his side of the net and told him not to talk like that about a friend of mine. He looked at me strangely and said, 'I'm talking about myself!' I agreed and then added, 'And aren't you a friend of mine?' He then told me he would keep quiet if I stayed on my side of the net. I am not sure if he understood my point but it occurred to me then that we often say things to ourselves that we would not say to our worst enemies. Interestingly, this could be seen as a form of arrogance because we are subtly saying that we can understand how mere mortals can make mistakes, but we are not in this category.

It is important that self-talk is realistic and positive. Being realistic means that self-talk is not about escaping from the events we have to face in life. Being positive means that self-talk can be a way of facing these events with more of our inner resources working for us. This task can begin by confronting some of the cognitive distortions we may be in the habit of using.

In writing about an inviting approach applied to oneself, Paula Helen Stanley (1992: 231–7) lists several distortions each of us may use from time to time in our inner speech. Here are some of the distortions we can attend to:

- *All-or-none thinking*: thinking things are either one way or another; you are either a success or a failure.
- *Overgeneralisation*: assuming too much from too little; if you were not successful at something once, you will never be successful at it.
- *Mental filtering*: selecting a small detail that confirms your inadequacy; seeing a slight sign of disapproval as a total rejection.
- *Mind reading*: believing you know what others are thinking about you; projecting your inadequate thoughts about yourself into the minds of others.
- *Fortune telling*: claiming to know what would happen if things were different; saying that if things were different there would be no problems.
- *Magnification*: overestimating the significance of an event; thinking that something that is important to you is important to everyone else.
- *Emotional reasoning*: using only what you initially feel to determine the truth of a situation; initial negative feelings are proof of inadequacy.
- *Labelling*: making global statements about yourself; using terms like 'total jerk' or 'loser' about yourself.
- *Personalisation*: thinking you are totally responsible for another's moods or actions; believing you are the total reason for another's problems.
- *Blaming*: thinking others are totally responsible for your moods or actions; believing they are the total reason for your problems.
- *Catastrophising*: increasing your anxiety by expecting the worst outcome; manufacturing fear through using 'what if' statements.
- *Double jeopardy*: becoming aware of your cognitive distortions and punishing yourself for having them.

Often enough, if we heard others making these distortions, we would easily recognise them and see their falsity. The real test is to apply this distortion detecting to ourselves.

Similar to medicine, the first rule of developing realistic and positive self-talk is to 'first do no harm'. The next step is to do some inviting things in the privacy of one's mind (Stanley, 1992: 237–9). These include the following:

- *Becoming an avid listener to your self-talk*: attending to what you say to yourself and how you say it.
- *Separating fact from fiction*: examining the evidence for your self-indictments.
- *Treating yourself with the same respect given to others*: internalising the basic kindness you offer others.
- *Using the reframe*: seeing if you can state something in the affirmative.
- *Avoiding the extremes*: becoming careful about using words like 'never' or 'always' when referring to your habits.
- *Getting a perceptual check*: asking others about their perception about something that happened or something you said or did.

These are some starting generalisations. For development to occur, these need to be applied to the conversations of our inner lives in kind but firm ways. Inviting ourselves personally depends on it.

Inviting personal wellness

Being in education for the long run means you have to attend to your health, growth and development. Because you cannot give what you do not have, it is important that you take care of what you have to give with – yourself. Taking care of yourself does not mean just avoiding illness or injury. It also involves a proactive stance towards wellness – the idea that you do not have to be sick to get better. This can be done in a systematic way by attending to five areas of one's life (Ardell, 1986):

- *Personal responsibility*: making it my life by deciding how I will respond to significant events outside and within me. This may mean disputing some of my negative and unrealistic self-talk and constructing more possibilities for flow experiences.
- *Nutritional awareness*: being aware of what one eats and why one is eating something. This means trying to achieve a generally healthy approach to food and finding ways to savour, understand and make better what enters your mouth.

- *Stress management*: being able to change distress to eustress, or positive stimulation (Seyle, 1974) and developing some skills of emotional intelligence (Goleman, 1995) in order to handle anger, depression and anxiety.
- *Physical fitness*: taking regular and enjoyable action with your body to develop strength, flexibility and endurance. Remembering that if you do not take care of your body, where will you live?
- *Environmental sensitivity*: becoming aware of the impact our environment has on us and the impact that we have on it. Becoming receptive to the more than human world we are encountering and the human effects on this world.

Orchestrating our personal lives for flow possibilities, realistic and positive self-talk and personal wellness are parts of the challenge of inviting oneself personally. As we pursue this task we also obtain a deeper understanding of what we are inviting others to do. Inviting educational leadership goes to the personal core of our existence by the imaginative acts of hope we use with ourselves.

Summary

- Personal life-management is a developmental process.
- Developing flow activities involves creatively orchestrating challenge and threat.
- Using realistic and positive self-talk is a way to move beyond self-defeating behaviour.
- Eliminating cognitive distortions frees oneself from unnecessary constraints.
- Inviting wellness is made up of personal responsibility, nutritional awareness, stress management, physical fitness and environmental sensitivity.
- If you do not take care of your body, where will you live?

Extending the conversation

Q: Why is it often easier to teach others what to do than to do it ourselves?

A: Words often just deal with the tip of the iceberg. Actions have to deal with the whole ice flow. Invitational leaders are aware of this and try to make their words deal with the whole experience. They also know the limitations of words and seek to try many things for themselves so they can learn to use words that call forth more possibilities.

Q: You have only given some starting points to orchestrating our personal lives. Is this enough?

A: Developing an educationally vibrant orchestrating self is a continuous process that should take a person into new areas of complexity. To give a formula for doing this reduces vibrancy to a mechanical process. Mechanical processing of the world can get in the way of leading for educational life.

Q: Flow sounds like New Age thinking. Does it have a scientific basis?

A: Mihalyi Csikszentmihalyi, who developed the concept of flow, is the former chair of the Department of Psychology at the University of Chicago. His work on flow is researched-based and has a grounding in cognitive psychology and phenomenology.

Q: Should we feel inadequate if are not experiencing flow in all our activities?

A: Seeking flow experiences is a goal because there are usually internal and external obstacles blocking its realisation. Feeling inadequate about not realising flow can become an obstacle to its realisation. Perhaps it is better to think of the realisation in terms of degrees rather than as an all-or-nothing achievement.

Q: I find myself rushed from one thing to another. Where can I find the time for flow activities?

A: The hectic pace of much of our life can certainly make achieving flow more difficult. At times we may have to reassess everything we are doing and decide if it is all necessary. Aiming to 'have it all' in the future is a way not to be able to savour the present. Not being able to savour the present will carry on in future presents. It takes a concerted effort to break this cycle.

Q: I cannot change the way I talk to myself. It's just the way I am. Why are you telling me I can?

A: Unless we think the voices we hear in our head are not our own, we can influence change. We have got into habits that are close to the centre of our subjective lives. These habits are not easily broken. Change can begin with an awareness of inner dialogue. Understanding the effects of what we are saying can move us to try new things to say. This can lead to new habits of self-talk.

Q: Won't this make a person too self-absorbed?

A: Self-absorbed means to care primarily about yourself and not attend to other aspects of the world. In contrast, attending to your self-talk can make you self-aware. This awareness can make it possible to remove obstacles from developing deeper connections with others and the world outside yourself.

Q: What does self-talk have to do with education?

A: Internal dialogue can make it easier or more difficult to learn something. If educational leaders can vocalise their productive internal dialogue at appropriate times they can model an important aspect of leading for educational life.

Q: Personal wellness sounds like good common sense. Where will I find the time to put it into practice?

A: It has been said that 'time is just a device to stop everything from happening at once'. If that is the case, then we have to use this device to stop too many things from happening in our lives. If you think of personal wellness as a sound investment in a higher quality of life now and in the future, then using time for it now should make sense.

Q: With all this attention to oneself, when will we deal with others?

A: I thought you would never ask. The next two chapters deal with our relationships with other individuals.

References

Ardell, D. (1986) *High Level Wellness: An Alternative, Doctors, Drugs, and Disease.* Berkeley, CA: Ten Speed Press.

Csikszentmihalyi, M. (1990) *Flow: The Psychology of Optimal Experience.* New York: HarperCollins.

Csikszentmihalyi, M. (1993) *The Evolving Self: A Psychology for the Third Millennium.* New York: HarperCollins.

Csikszentmihalyi, M. (1997) *Finding Flow: The Psychology of Engagement with Everyday Life.* New York: HarperCollins.

Goleman, D. (1995) *Emotional Intelligence.* New York: Bantam.

Jacobs, J. (2001) *The Nature of Economies.* Toronto: Vintage Canada.

Purkey, W.W. (2000) *What Students Say to Themselves: Internal Dialogue and School Success.* Thousand Oaks, CA: Corwin Press.

Seyle, H. (1974). *Stress Without Distress.* New York: Signet.

Stanley, P.H. (1992) 'Inviting things to do in the privacy of your own mind' in Novak, J.M. (ed.) *Advancing Invitational Thinking.* San Francisco: Caddo Gap Press, 221–42.

5
■ ■ ■

Interpersonal Leadership

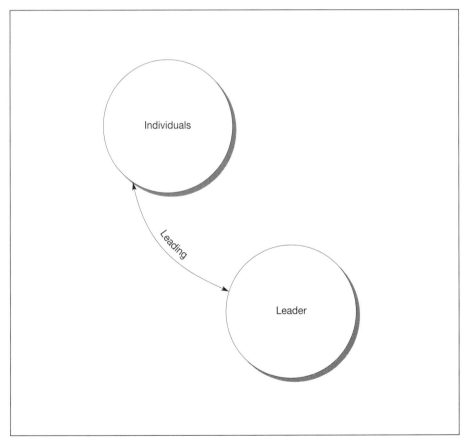

Figure 5.1: Interpersonal leadership

Being inviting with others begins with a perceptual orientation that is translated into an inviting stance. Developing an inviting stance enables an educational leader to establish a doing-with relationship with others. Focusing on the craft of inviting provides educators with a systematic way to become intentionally inviting.

What is involved in communicating with another individual?

How do you put good intentions into practice when others are involved?

What is needed to establish a doing-with relationship?

Can we get better at the process of relating to others?

Because of the quality of relationships needed for ethical interactions, these are essential questions needed to keep educational living alive. This chapter is *unlikely* to connect with your beliefs if you:

- think trust can be mandated;
- believe that leadership is mostly about badgering and bartering;
- feel that you either have a knack for working with others or you don't;
- think that leading others is like stuffing olives.

This chapter is more *likely* to connect with your beliefs if you:

- think that developing trust is a delicate and precarious endeavour;
- believe that leadership is about mutuality;
- feel that people can get better at working with others;
- think that leading others is like dancing.

Inviting educational leadership is contained in the quality of human relationships necessary to appreciate each person in the present and call forth his or her potential. Emphasising the perceptual nature of human relationships, this chapter looks at the dynamics of developing an inviting stance that enables one to operate at an intentionally inviting level.

Perceiving human interaction

But if I am only for myself, what am I?

(Hillel)

Human interaction is dialogic not monologic. Because each person has a perceptual field filled with present sensations, memories, anticipations, habits and desires, human interaction can be a complex affair. Rather than operating in a linear, mechanical fashion, people come to terms with each other through symbols and referents.

For example, when Person X sends a message to Person Y, it does not go mechanically from the first person's perceptual field to the second person's perceptual field (*see* Figure 5.2). Only on *Star Trek* do people mindwrite and mindread with one another's perceptual fields. Here on earth human messages move in a more roundabout manner because each person is an encoder and decoder emersed in a social world filled with potential meanings (Percy, 1983). A way to describe this dialogical process is given in Figure 5.3. Here we have Person X encoding a message through symbols with referents to Person Y. Person Y decodes the symbols and connects them to referents in his or her perceptual field and infers an intention to Person X. In the process of decoding a message, Person Y is sending a message back to Person X, and the process continues. Because each person is not a blank slate and has memories of previous interactions and expectations for future outcomes, the complexity of the interaction can increase exponentially. It is sometimes a wonder we can communicate at all.

The senders of a message do not have control over the ways other people may interpret the message sent. To act as if they do have control over the interpretation of the message sent is to act in an impositional of dictatorial manner. However, the senders of a message do have control over the position from which they operate and can work with others to understand better how they interpret the messages they receive. This dialogical process works with integrity when it is authentically connected with some basic helping perceptions and embodied in an inviting stance.

Helping perceptions

Inviting educational leadership is rooted in a perceptual approach to working with people. Building on the Snygg-Combs theory of perception (Snygg and Combs, 1949; Combs and Snygg, 1959; Combs, Richards and Richards, 1976), it emphasises understanding others and working with them as they see themselves and the situations they are in. This approach has been revised several times and applied to teacher education (Combs, 1982; Combs, Blume, Newman and Wass, 1974) and helping relationships (Combs, Avila and Purkey, 1978; Combs and Gonzalez, 1997).

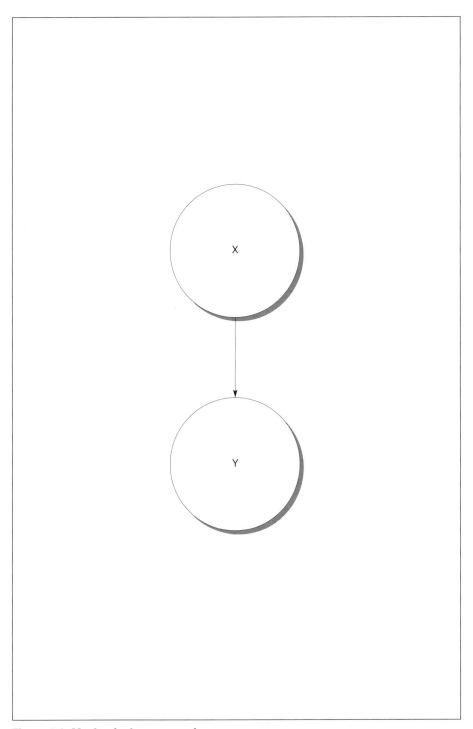

Figure 5.2: Mechanical programming

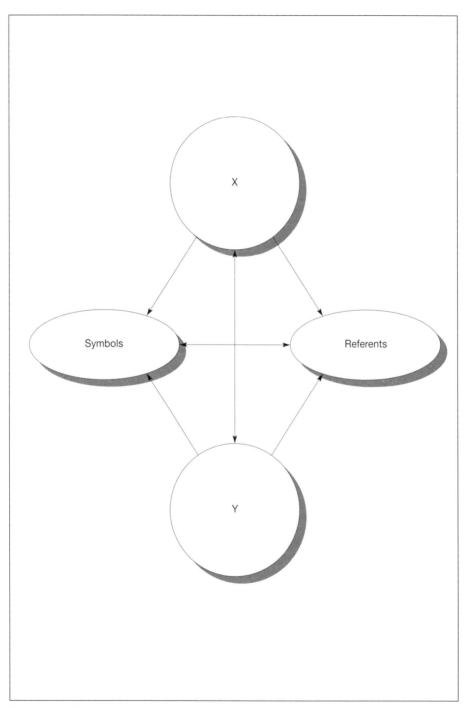

Figure 5.3: Human communication
(*Source*: Percy, 1983)

In an early distillation of Combs's research, Wasicsko (1977) reported four important perceptual characteristics of effective helpers. He noted that they saw themselves, others, purpose and frame of reference in the following ways:

- *Themselves*: identified rather than unidentified. They felt connected with those they were working with; they tended to think of others in terms of 'us' rather than 'they'.
- *Others*: able rather than unable. They viewed others as able to learn important things; they tended to think in terms of how they could build on others' interests and ways of making sense of the world.
- *Purpose*: people-oriented rather than things-oriented. They focused on people's thoughts and feelings and modified rules and procedures accordingly.
- *Frame of reference*: long-term rather than short-term. They had a long-range perspective and tended to think of the life-effects of learning rather than covering material or going through procedures.

This perceptual orientation gives helpers a sense of empathy, efficacy, focus and perspective. When it is connected with a life stance, a habitual way of interacting, it enables leaders to become more intentionally inviting.

Developing an inviting stance

Working with others in inviting ways is like playing tennis. First, in tennis there is a net you are not allowed to cross. On your side of the net you have control of what you do. When the ball is on the other person's side, it is in their control. Second, in tennis a player prepares for each shot by taking a stance towards the ball. This stance, although individual, follows certain principles that give the player proper focus and leverage. However, even the best stance does not guarantee that the player will win the point. It does, however, make it easier for the player to make solid contact with the ball. Since inviting others is a dialogical process in which we cannot go over the net, control of others is not the goal. When the communication is in your court, the goal is to make solid contact. If you do this, the points will take care of themselves.

Helping perceptions of self, others, purpose and frame of reference are put into practice by developing an inviting stance that respects the net and enables a leader to focus and use appropriate leverage. This inviting stance has the following five characteristics (*see* Figure 5.4):

Figure 5.4: The inviting stance

- *Care*. This is the glue that holds the stance together. The inviting approach is about extending the caring impulse (Noddings, 1984). This caring impulse is manifested by displaying full receptivity to the other and seeking to further the other person's educational purposes. This is done by de-centring oneself and listening for the interests and meanings expressed by the other. If someone cannot work at doing this, it is difficult to believe that he or she feels identified with others or sees them as able to learn important things.

- *Trust*. The inviting approach stresses the fundamental interdependence of people. People are seen as unique parts of a living system of messages, with their development linked to the genuineness, reliability, truthfulness and competence of those around them. Developing and sustaining an inviting stance is about establishing a trustworthy pattern of interaction over time. When trust is lacking, everything is called into question. People are at cross-purposes and time, energy and potential are lost and not easily restored.

- *Respect*. The importance of not 'crossing the net' is what makes invitational education dialogical. This means recognising each person's ability to accept, reject, hold in abeyance and negotiate the messages sent their way. It also involves an appreciation of each person's uniqueness and participation in meaningful groups. At a basic level, this commits an inviting leader to fight practices that embarrass, insult, humiliate or subject others to pre-judice. Feeling that you have been 'dissed' by another is a recurring issue in a multicultural society.

- *Intentionality*. The inviting stance is about being responsible and self-correcting in one's actions. By being intentional, leaders have a direction in which they are going and are able to work to develop the persistence and resourcefulness to get there by a variety of methods. This links with the perception of having a large frame of reference and being people-oriented. As leaders, this intentionality also means an emphasis on being pro-active and self-correcting in one's actions.

- *Optimism*. The inviting stance is a hopeful approach to working with people. This hope is not a belief that good things are bound to happen, but rather the realistic assessment that good things have a better chance of occurring if one approaches them in a positive, open and thoughtful manner. With such a mindset, a leader has a wider horizon of meanings available to work with and so has more possibilities for calling forth successful outcomes.

The inviting stance is a manifestation of a theory of practice that aims to put perceptions to work. This stance is more likely to develop when it is systematically applied to the craft of inviting.

The craft of inviting

The inviting approach aims to blend heart, head and hands. Perceptions get to the heart of the matter, a consistent stance gets a leader heading in the right direction, and the development of the craft of inviting enables a person to handle ever more complex situations. The craft of inviting involves a cluster of skill grouped around three phases: being ready; doing with; and following through.

Being ready

Being intentional means doing things on purpose for purposes one can defend. The thoughtful, pro-active nature of inviting takes place even before a person comes in contact with others. It takes place in the way people prepare the environment and prepare themselves:

- *Preparing the environment.* How we handle the area we work in sends important messages to others. Creating a people-friendly work area that is clean, comfortable and free from interruptions sends the message that people matter and you want them to feel at ease. A lively environment contains live things like plants, colourful artwork and good smells – educators have been known to microwave spiced apples to produce a home-like aroma in classrooms and offices. Also, having refreshments available so people can 'break bread' together is a way to begin a meeting in a relaxed way and to share some healthy food – educators have been known to have supplies of bottled water they share with others, beginning their meetings with a toast. Imaginative acts of hope begin with the design of hopeful settings.

- *Preparing oneself.* The inviting approach is centred on thoughtful action. Perhaps more deeply, though, it has its core in reflected feeling. Remembering what is was like to be disinvited and invited in one's own schooling experience is a way to focus oneself to be receptive to others. Imagining what we want our students, co-workers, supervisors and community members to remember from their encounters with us can be a means for us to focus on what is important in our interaction with them. Preparing oneself also means confronting one's prejudices and blind spots. Reflecting on ways we have grown and thinking about ways we would like to grow in our understanding of others makes us realise we have come a long way but there is still some distance to travel.

Doing with

When we are actually in contact with other individuals, the quality of the relationship is enhanced if we attend to some basic features of good communication. The following seven factors enable leaders to show thoughtful respect for the interpersonal processes necessary to have a more lasting effect on others.

- *Developing goodwill.* As a doing-with process, invitational leadership is dependent on good feelings between people. These good feelings between people often take time to develop and can be negated by not respecting the confidential nature of most communications, being judgemental, or not following through on previous agreements. In addition, one's body language can sometimes be unintentionally disinviting. Tone of voice, facial expression, body stance and gestures may communicate that we are not at ease with a person or situation. Getting feedback from friends can be a way to become aware of things of which we were previously unaware. Also, the use of appropriate disclosure can be a way to communicate that 'we are in this together'.

- *Reaching a variety of people.* In sports there is a propensity to practise what you are already good at. Similarly in interpersonal relations people have a tendency to communicate with those who are most like them. Leaders, however, need to connect with a variety of people to become better informed and avoid being perceived as being exclusive or having favourites. This is done by being systematic in sending invitations to others – one way is to use checklists to note those you may not have connected with recently. Teachers and administators have found that a card catalogue with the names of people in their institution can be a way to become aware of those who may have been previously neglected.

- *Reading situations.* The perceptual nature of inviting means going beneath behaviour to the meaning of the behaviour. This means paying attention to the context of what is going on and being able to see what is happening from the viewpoint of the people involved.

Often when people say they do not care, what they may really be saying is that they do not want to be hurt. Also, when people may be showing agreement they may not, in fact, understand what they are agreeing to or what their agreement may imply. By probing situations for personal meanings to the participants, invitational possibilities are opened up.

- *Making invitations attractive*. Invitations are extended for the sake of being accepted. Recipients are more apt to be open to accepting an invitation if they perceive that the extender of the invitation has taken the time and interest to extend a thoughtful invitation. This means not having a 'one size fits all style' but rather showing a sensitivity to the uniqueness of the person you are working with and having a variety of possible invitations to use. This is especially true in using praise. Many people are rightfully sceptical of global praise. What they may be open to is private recognition of something into which they have put a good deal of effort. To show that you have noticed something that is meaningful to another person is to show that you think they are doing worthwhile things.

- *Ensuring delivery*. Invitations are more than perceptions and more than a stance. They are messages that are intended to get delivered. It is the responsibility of the extender of the invitation to see that it is sent, received and acknowledged. Being clear about what is invited lets the recipient know what is being agreed to when, where and how. Being clear about an invitation also gives the extender of the invitation a better understanding of whether it is accepted or, if not, why it may have been rejected. This understanding of the reason for declining an invitation enables the extender to restate the invitation or try other invitations.

- *Negotiating alternatives*. There is no guarantee that an invitation will be accepted. It depends on the co-operation and goodwill of the participants. As a dialogical process, the sender determines the rules for extending the invitation. It is up to the receiver to determine the rules for acceptance. These rules are negotiable and open to new possibilities. The negotiation of alternatives is not the broken-record repetition of the same invitation over and over again, but the imaginative amending or resubmitting of a more acceptable invitation. A simple technique that may get to the heart of the issue is to ask the other person, 'If you will not accept this invitation, let me know one that you will accept'. In many cases this will get to the heart of the issue.

- *Handling rejection*. The inviting process is open-ended in that the recipient can accept, reject, negotiate or hold in abeyance the invitation extended. It is not written that even the best invitation will be accepted. This can hurt. Leaders may wonder why they should use this approach when it may leave them vulnerable. First, however, they need to decide if an invitation was truly rejected. Sometimes a recipient may want more time to think about an invitation and how and when to accept it. That being said, there are times when an invitation is clearly and unmistakably being rejected. When this occurs, it is important to realise that the rejection of an invitation is not the same as the rejection of the person. People may have a variety of reasons for rejecting an invitation that have nothing to do with the person who extended the invitation. The rejected invitation may, however, make it easier for the person to accept other invitations.

Following through

The inviting process begins on the extender's side of the net and then moves to the recipient's side. The process ends on the extender's side, where the invitation will be completed and the process reflected upon.

- *Completing the invitation.* If an invitation is accepted it is the ethical responsibility of the extender to make sure that what was offered is made available. Not to follow through on an invitation can be doubly disinviting – it tells the recipient that he or she is not valuable enough for you to finish up what was agreed to and that he or she was foolish enough to believe you. Such unethical cases, in which action does not follow the words, makes it difficult for people to accept other's invitations. Because of this ethical responsibility to follow-through on an invitation, it is important to be clear on what is being invited and what is necessary to complete the invitation. This is why it is important to invite educative experiences in one's own life so one can have a sense of what one is inviting others to do.

- *Reflecting on the process.* If an invitation is accepted and responsibly followed through on, the experience should be savoured. This is what education is all about. Moments like this should be brought up later and used as a reminder of the educational successes one has had. If an invitation was not accepted, it should be used as a learning experience and examined in terms of what may have happened. Was the invitation unclear or inappropriate? Did the recipient have the skills or interest to accept the invitation? What might I do differently? Who might I discuss this with? Since the inviting approach is an evolving theory of practice, the most important question might be: what have I learned about myself and others?

The concept of inviting others to participate in educational living is a simple idea that takes educators into more complex situations. It involves embodying educational commitments in a personal stance and tactfully putting them into practice. It means using and extending many dimensions of one's personality and having the courage to face rejection. Simple (meaning to get to the heart of an idea) does not mean it is easy. It should mean, however, it is worth the effort if one wishes to get to the essence of developing humans' resources.

Summary

- To work with people in an ethical way, human interaction needs to be understood dialogically not monologically.
- Invitational leaders pay attention to how people interpret events.
- Good helpers possess people-oriented perceptions of themselves, others, purpose and frame of reference.
- An inviting stance is centred in care and includes trust, respect, intentionality and optimism.
- The craft of inviting involves being ready, doing-with and following through.
- Being ready to invite means preparing the environment and oneself.
- Doing-with includes developing trust, reaching each person, reading situations, making invitations attractive, ensuring delivery, negotiating, and handling rejection.
- Following through means to complete the invitation, savour the experience and reflect on the process.

Extending the conversation

Q: To say the inviting is dialogic sounds like more educational jargon. Why use the term?

A: Distinctions can make a difference. The approach used in this book is that human beings should be looked at as people who need to be understood, not objects that are merely to be stimulated and reinforced. The word 'dialogic' represents this sensibility and can deepen our understanding of the nature of a 'doing-with' relationship.

Q: How can you be certain of what is in another person's perceptual field?

A: We can never be certain of what is in another's perceptual field. What we can do is to work to understand how they might see things and find ways to develop some shared perceptions.

Q: How do you get basic helping perceptions?

A: The basic helping perceptions are not something that a person is born with or has once and for all times. Rather, they should be thought of as achievements that need continually to be re-examined. By 'trying on' these perceptions and applying them to educational situations, educational leaders can begin to develop their own unique variation. Perceptions are beliefs that can be made deeper by persistent application and reflection.

Q: Isn't seeing people as able just mind over grey matter?

A: Seeing people as able is not wishful thinking but rather an attempt to focus on what they can do in the present and what they might need to do next to improve. If we did not think people could learn something important, why would we ever try to teach them anything?

Q: When we have so much material to cover, how can we think in terms of the long term?

A: If we do not think in terms of the long run we are short-changing our students. We have an ethical responsibility as educators to have our students become life-long learners. Teaching them important material is a way to do that. Could you imagine a doctor saying to a patient, 'I am unable to give you the operation you need. However, I can give you this other quicker operation that actually might make you worse'?

Q: I care, but I work in a school where others do not care. What can I do?

A: People always care about something. It is necessary to find out what they care about and build on that. Also, if we want to improve other people we must first work to improve ourselves.

Q: How can I trust others when they have deceived me?

A: Trust is not an all-or-nothing endeavour. If trust has been destroyed it needs to be rebuilt in small doses. Although being deceived is a bad thing, never being able to trust may be a worse thing. There will always be risk in trusting, but there is greater risk in never trusting.

Q: How can I be optimistic in times like this?

A: The times we live in are always ambiguous. That is, they always possess both negative and positive actualities and possibilities. The challenge is to build on the positive and work to eliminate the negative. The times are always changing. It is the job of educational leaders to bring about positive changes.

Q: How can anybody follow all of the steps of the craft of inviting?

A: The steps of the craft of inviting do not have to be followed exactly in all the situations we encounter. The steps point to possible points of intervention and show the systematic thinking that may be necessary to become intentionally inviting. You do not have to be perfect, just want to get better and enjoy the process as you grow.

Q: Is there a danger of being seen as weak if I try to be too inviting?

A: Inviting behaviour is strong not weak. Anyone can yell, scream or attack. It takes strength to work intelligently to sustain imaginative acts of hope. It takes strength to treat others with respect and expect respect in return.

Q: Aren't there just some people you will never get through to?

A: Perhaps, but how do you know if you never try?

Q: This inviting stuff is not so easy then?

A: Let's see how it gets even more difficult in the next chapter.

References

Combs, A.W. (1982) *A Personal Approach to Teaching: Beliefs that Make a Difference*. Boston: Allyn and Bacon.

Combs, A.W., Avila, D. and Purkey, W.W. (1978) *Helping Relationships: Basic Concepts for the Helping Professionals*. 2nd edn. Boston: Allyn and Bacon.

Combs, A.W., Blume, R.A., Newman, A.J. and Wass, H.L. (1974) *The Professional Education of Teachers: A Humanistic Approach to Teacher Preparation*. 2nd edn. Boston: Allyn and Bacon.

Combs, A.W. and Gonzalez, D.M. (1997) *Helping Relationships: Basic Concepts for the Helping Professionals*. 4th edn. Boston: Allyn and Bacon.

Combs, A.W., Richards, A.C. and Richards, F. (1976) *Perceptual Psychology: A Humanistic Approach to the Study of Persons*. New York: Harper and Row.

Combs, A.W. and Snygg, D. (1959) *Individual Behavior: A Perceptual Approach to Behavior*. 2nd edn. New York: Harper and Row.

Noddings, N. (1984) *Caring: A Feminine Approach to Ethics and Moral Education*. Berkeley, CA: University of California Press.

Percy, W. (1983) *Lost in the Cosmos: The Last Self-Help Book*. New York: Simon and Schuster.

Snygg, D. and Combs, A.W. (1949) *Individual Behavior: A New Frame of Reference for Psychology*. New York: Harper and Row.

Wasicsko, M.M. (1977) 'The Effects of Training and Perceptual Orientation on the Reliability of Perceptual Inferences for Selecting Effective Teachers'. Unpublished doctoral dissertation. University of Florida, Gainesville.

6
■ ■ ■

Managing
Conflict

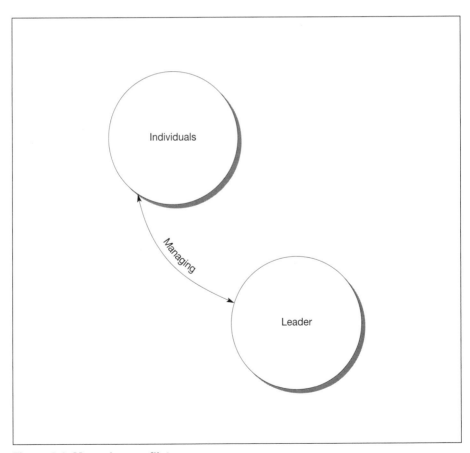

Figure 6.1: Managing conflict

Inviting educational leaders understand that conflict with individuals is a natural part of life and can be managed in principled, growth-producing ways. Fighting fire with water is preferred to adding combustibles to potentially flammable situations. Moving to learning conversations can be a way to grow through philosophical differences.

Is conflict to be avoided at all costs?

Can conflict be managed in principled ways?

Do people really want to work things out?

Do we have to pretend to agree with individuals with whom we disagree?

Because of the prudence needed to handle difficult situations, these are essential questions that need to be asked to enable educators to grow as they handle difficult situations. This chapter is *unlikely* to connect with your beliefs if you:

- think conflict should always be avoided;
- believe nothing good can come from conflict;
- feel that every conflict should be dealt with immediately;
- think you have to pretend to agree with others a lot.

This chapter is more *likely* to connect with your beliefs if you:

- think conflict is a natural part of life;
- believe conflict can be a source of growth;
- feel that some issues need time for sober second thought;
- think that human conflict often involves dealing with shades of grey.

Inviting others is easy when the sun is shining and everything is going your way. People have caring relations with one another and trust abounds. However, in a fast-paced, multicultural, postmodern world filled with more than 6 billion individuals, this euphoric state is not always evident. Clouds often block the sun and people bump into one another and have conflicts about what happened and what should be happening. This chapter deals with managing conflict in inviting and effective ways. It introduces methods for dealing with interpersonal concerns and philosophical differences.

Interpersonal concerns

Even invitational leaders have to deal with troublesome situations. Concerns will not go away just because a person practises the craft of inviting. A key question for invitational leaders is 'Can concerns with individuals be handled in ways that coincide with the principles of the inviting stance and still be effective?' With this aim in mind, the 'rule of the six Cs' was developed (Purkey and Novak, 1996; Novak and Purkey, 2001). This straightforward method for dealing with concerns seeks to deal with them:

- *At the lowest possible emotional level*: operating at higher emotional levels can mean more restricted perceptual fields.
- *With the least expense of energy*: aren't there better things to do with one's time?
- *In an appropriate and caring manner*: staying true to inviting principles represents invitational integrity.
- *In a potentially growth producing way*: finding a way to cultivate the educational value of any experience is a habit that can be practised.

The six Cs are concern, confer, consult, confront, combat and conciliate. The rule is to start with the lowest possible C and use it as thoroughly as possible and only move up to a higher C as necessary. Anybody can throw petrol on a fire and transform a spark into a major conflagration. It takes understanding and skill to manage the heat at the lowest possible level. Let us examine each of the Cs.

Concern

It is important to determine first whether an action is really necessary in a potential conflict situation. At this point it is helpful to ask oneself, 'Is this a matter for concern or is this a preference?' A preference is something we would like to see happen. A concern deals with something that needs to happen if we are to remain respectful to ourselves, professional or ethical in our practice. Here are some questions that help to determine whether a situation really is a matter of concern:

- Will this situation take care of itself without my intervention?
- Is this the proper time for me to be concerned with this?
- Is this one of the inevitable tensions and opportunities that occurs in a pluralistic, democratic society?
- What might I need to know about what is happening?
- Does this concern a legal, moral or safety issue?

The world can often revolve without our help. Many situations will take care of themselves at this level. However, there are times when a situation is sufficiently troublesome and requires more than a sober second thought. It is then time to move to the next C.

Confer

A professional educator should be able to do more than the average layperson when it comes to working with people for educational purposes. If this were not the case, then there would be no need for professionals and professional training. Invitational leaders seek to invite voluntary compliance with reasonable rules. It is difficult to do this if you are out of control yourself. The conferring process begins by first calming oneself and then demonstrating self-control throughout the conference.

To confer is to initiate an informal conversation in private. During this private meeting, the inviting leader should be relaxed and non-threatening with the other person and be able to state in a respectful and caring way what the concern is, why it is a concern, and what is proposed to resolve the concern. The next step is to get voluntary compliance from the other person. A way to do this is to use a method called 'three plusses and a wish'. For example, you may wish to confer with a colleague who has been using your transparencies and not returned them. You might say to the colleague, 'You are a respected and creative teacher and I enjoy working with you *and* when you take my transparencies I do not have them available for my teaching. Could you please ask first before you use them? Will you do this for me?' The reason why 'and' was used rather than 'but' is because people have a tendency to disregard everything that precedes a 'but'. Asking for, and obtaining, verbal compliance is important at this stage, and later, should there be movement to a higher level.

Here are some questions to ask oneself about conferring:

- Have I respectfully expressed my concern?
- Have I honestly listened to what the other person said?
- Have I found out anything new about this situation?
- Did I ask for and receive voluntary compliance?

When used patiently and with good faith, conferring will enable a leader to manage many difficult situations. If it does not work, it is time to move to the next C.

Consult

The move after conferring is to a more formal stage. At the consultation stage the leader reminds the other person what had been previously agreed upon and the fact that the agreement has not been kept. The leader then listens to what the other person has to say. An offer may be made to assist the person in keeping the agreement and some brainstorming may occur or suggestions made. Here are some questions that might be of assistance at this stage:

- Have I clarified what is expected?
- Have I been open to new information that may change the situation?
- How can I help the other person abide by the agreement?
- Have I thought about the consequences of not resolving the conflict?

If the troublesome situation has not been resolved, it is time to move to the next C.

Confront

The confrontation stage is a serious, no-nonsense attempt to resolve the concern. While still operating from an inviting stance, the leader will point out that the concern has been previously and repeatedly addressed, with the other person giving his or her word to make the necessary changes, and yet, the situation has not changed. Now it is important to state the consequences that will follow if the other person does not live up to the agreement. Here are some questions to ask at this stage to prevent escalation:

- Have I made an honest attempt to manage the conflict at a lower level?
- Do I have documented evidence to show previous efforts? (It may be necessary to begin documenting at the consulting stage.)
- Do I have sufficient power to follow-through with the consequences?
- Do I have sufficient will to follow-through with the consequences?

If you have been sincere in your previous attempts and the consequences are fair and respectful, then it is time to move to the next level.

Combat

The word 'combat' is used here as a verb not a noun. It means to reduce or eliminate a situation, not a person. It represents a serious stage in which one uses direct, immediate and firm action to move on the stated consequences. At this level, because of the emotion that may be involved, the results may be unpredictable. This, along with the time and energy it takes to combat a tense situation, means that one should enter this level very carefully. Here are some questions to ask at this level:

- Is there room for any other solution?
- Have I sought help from other colleagues or outside sources?
- Do I have support and resources to combat the situation?
- Can I publicly defend my actions?

Invitational leaders are still expected to use an inviting stance at this level. Respectful treatment is still the rule. After the consequences have been applied, it is time to go to the next C.

Conciliate

It is important not to end in a combat mode. There is a need to return to a state of normality. This means that former combatants and non-combatants need to find ways to reflect on and possibly grow as a result of what has happened. This conciliating stage is guided by three rules. First, do not fan the flames of tension. Second, give people some space. In-your-face types of leadership are not appropriate when attempting to bring people together. Third, 'keep dancing with the one you brought to the dance'. That is, stick with the principles and practices that you have been using throughout the process. Here are some questions that are important to ask at this level:

- Have I avoided rubbing it in?
- Have I given people time and space to resume normal interactions?
- Can I use some helpful intermediaries?
- Will I return to the first C when a new concern occurs?

The rule of the six Cs can be a way to manage conflicts at lower levels of emotional intensity. In doing so a leader will save time and energy and reduce hostility and acrimony. Will it work all the time? No. However, in the spirit of invitational optimism, it can be a way to manage more conflicts in a better way and one can get better as a result of the experience. Getting better as a result of learning from experience is an important part of inviting educational leadership. This growth can even occur in dealing with philosophical differences.

Inviting philosophical differences

When our daughter was 11 years old, we were going up a two-person ski lift. Thinking I had a captive audience (we were 50 feet above the ground), I thought this would be a good place to explain to her the philosopher John Dewey's concept of continuity and interaction. I explained how everything that has happened up until now has led up to what is happening now, and what we do now will affect the rest of the future. Her first response was silence (I thought maybe she was in a state of winter contemplation or else was ignoring me). After a few seconds, she said, 'Perhaps'. Then a few seconds later she added, 'Upon reflection, we could all get sucked into a black hole and it will not matter what we do'. I was silent for a few seconds, being surprised both by the method she used and the ideas she expressed. After a few seconds of silence, I responded to her and said, 'Perhaps'. A few seconds later, following her lead, I added, 'Upon reflection, what we do matters at least for now, and that should count for something'. Our conversation continued on the next ski lift.

This was an important conversation for me for many reasons. Relating to managing conflict, it pointed to a method for dealing with philosophical differences with the spirit of inviting educational reflection. This method:

- demonstrates respect for the other person;
- shows you have taken his or her ideas seriously;
- allows you to state your position honestly;
- invites the possibility of mutually developing a more integrative framework.

Here are the four steps of the method:

1 *Silence*. Philosophical issues require some thought. To respond immediately may imply that you have not really heard what the other person said or you think the comment can be handled with an off-the-cuff remark.

2 *Perhaps*. This communicates to the other person that he or she may be correct, but you are not really sure. You want some more time to think about it.

3 *Upon reflection*. After giving the matter some thought, you state what you agree with and what you have difficulty with.

4 *What do you think*? You put the ball back in the other's court and the conversation continues as you both work to find a more complex principle to handle the differences.

Let us see what this method would look like in the following conversation. A colleague tells you that today's students have it a lot easier than students did when he was young.

1 You are silent for at least three seconds.

2 You say, 'Perhaps'.

3 After three more seconds you may say, 'Upon reflection, it may be true that students have more conveniences available to them' *and* you also think they have to deal with a more complex and ambiguous world.

4 You add, 'What do you think?' The other person may agree with both statements and together you may decide that each generation has its advantages and disadvantages and needs to find meaningful ways to make sense of them.

Will this work in all cases? Of course not. This is an idealised view of a conversation. It does, however, point to possibilities for mutual exploration that can turn two 'Nos' into a larger 'Yes'. That's what imaginative acts of hope are about when working with individuals.

Summary

- The rule of the six Cs aims to handle conflicts at the lowest level, with the least energy, and with growth producing possibilities.
- A concern differs from a preference in that it can involve a sense of safety, legality or morality.
- When conferring, use 'three plusses and a wish'.
- When consulting, remind the person of previous agreements.
- When confronting, state the consequences of the other continuing a line of behaviour.
- To combat a situation, follow through on the consequences previously stated.
- During conciliation, do not 'fan the flames'.
- Philosophical differences can be ways to understand and explore contrasting perspectives.

Extending the conversation

Q: Are invitational leaders trying to avoid conflict?

A: Invitational leaders realise that there will always be conflict in complex human endeavours (and in simple endeavours also). What they want to avoid are destructive conflicts – conflicts that do emotional and social damage. By having a principled way to deal effectively with conflicts, leaders can often turn conflicts into potential grow situations.

Q: Is it easy to tell the difference between a preference and a concern?

A: Sometimes it can be. For example, if it is a matter of safety, legality or morality, it is usually clearly a matter of concern. However, deciding if it is one of these three is not always so easy. Perhaps another way to think about this is to ask: 'If I do nothing in this situation, what will happen?' If the consequences are insignificant, it might only be a preference.

Q: Don't people get suspicious when you give them three plusses before your wish?

A: They certainly will if that is the only time you are positive with them. However, if you are affirmative on a regular basis, then they are more likely to work with you when there is a concern.

Q: Doesn't it take too much time to follow the rule of the six Cs?

A: The six Cs should be used in appropriate doses. Starting with the first step should save time because many difficult issues will be settled there. There is an elementary school in North Carolina that taught the six Cs to its students and it claims it spends less time on discipline problems now.

Q: Is 'combat' too violent a word to use with invitational leadership?

A: 'Combat' is used as a verb, not a noun. It means to remove a situation, not a person. Even in the most inviting situations, strong action may need to be taken. The important thing is not to lead with it, because if you are not successful, you have run out of moves.

Q: Can conflicting situations ever be the same after they have been combatted?

A: They may never be the same but they can sometimes be better, because a respectful process has been followed and there has been a change from which people have learned.

Q: Do people really want to discuss philosophical differences?

A: Often they do if discussions are handled with care and respect. Educational leaders work to promote such discussions.

Q: Are people all that matter in education?

A: People are a part of all aspects of education and so interpersonal communication will always be important. However, it is not all there is. It is time to move on to consider values and knowledge.

References

Novak, J.M. and Purkey, W.W. (2001) *Invitational Education.* Bloomington, IN: Phi Delta Kappa.

Purkey, W.W. and Novak, J.M. (1996). *Inviting School Success: A Self-Concept Approach to Teaching, Learning, and Democratic Practice.* 3rd edn. Belmont, CA: Wadsworth.

7

■ ■ ■

Leading for Values and Knowledge

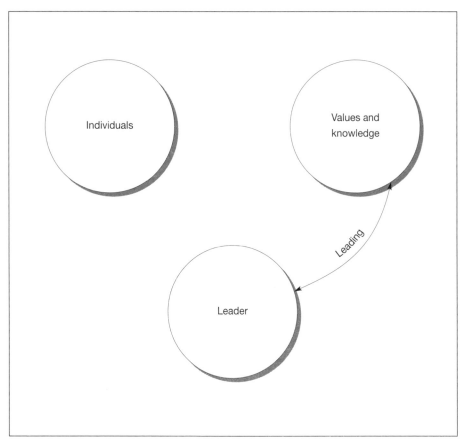

Figure 7.1: Leading for values and knowledge

> Inviting educational leaders care about what is taught and learned in schools. They invite a healthy self-concept-as-learner and disciplined minds to understand the world of and for knowledge.
>
> *What kinds of learning are valued?*
>
> *How important is it for students to learn to think about important issues?*
>
> *Do academic disciplines matter?*
>
> *Is it important for students to see themselves as learners?*

Because of the reflection necessary for important learning to take place, these are questions that need to be asked as educational leaders grow through the teaching– learning process. This chapter is *unlikely* to connect with your beliefs if you:

- think the good, the true and the beautiful are irrelevant to education;
- believe that cognition should be separated from affect;
- feel that student self-concept has no place in education;
- think that education is basically about getting good test scores.

This chapter is more *likely* to connect with your beliefs if you:

- think students need to examine issues of importance;
- believe that cognition and affect are vitally linked;
- feel it is important that students learn that they can learn;
- think test scores are only a small part of an education.

'Invite' is a transitive verb. It needs an object to complete its meaning. People are invited to something. For invitational leaders, people are invited to learn to savour, understand and better more of their experiences. This is more likely to happen if people feel good about themselves as learners and participate in a community of enquirers. This chapter looks at inviting others professionally by focusing on self-concept-as-learner and the types of learning that helps bring this about.

Self-concept-as-learner

Inviting educational leadership values people, knowledge and democratic relationships. It is about cordially summoning people to realise more of their potential and to use their best knowledge and deepest values meaningfully to participate in and extend democratic practices. By focusing on self-concept-as-learner, educators can work to attain these goals.

The Florida Key has been a useful tool for examining self-concept-as-learner in a variety of settings (Purkey, Cage and Graves, 1973; Harper and Purkey, 1993; Finger, 1995). It offers four areas on which educational leaders can focus: relating, asserting, investing and coping. An examination of each of these factors can suggest ways that an educational leader may be professionally inviting with others.

Relating

As indicated by the Florida Key, students who relate well are more likely to trust, appreciate and identify with their classmates, teachers and school. They are able to get along with others and have a relaxed approach to what is going on around them. An important part of inviting educational leadership is to encourage more and more people to be a part of the larger 'we' that is being constructed. This means finding ways to involve those who may be overlooked or ignored in professional and social activities. Especially important in a multicultural setting is the removal of unintentionally disinviting barriers that divide people into the informed inner circle and the marginalised outer circle. If the inviting stance means we are all in this together, relating is an important vehicle for making this happen. A vibrantly interactive classroom and school are not noisy distractions but vital necessities for learning.

Asserting

Assertion lies between aggression and acquiescence. To aggress is to try to meet your needs while disregarding the needs of others. To acquiesce is to disregard your needs and give in to the needs of others. Assertion, however, is an attempt to meet your needs while still respecting the needs of others. When applied to learning, assertion refers to the degree of control a person has over a situation. Those who can assert themselves do not feel that learning possibilities are out of reach, while those low in asserting have a sense of learned helplessness (Seligman, 1991), a sense that any action is futile. Inviting educational leaders promote democratic decision making and moral reasoning as a way to encourage asserting behaviour. They work in schools that encourage all people to assert themselves in socially appropriate ways.

Promoting assertive behaviour means taking seriously the idea that people are valuable, able and responsible.

Investing

Investing deals with a willingness to try new things, to look at situations in different ways and to explore unexplored ways of thinking. People who demonstrate this trait are rewarded by the enjoyment of the activity itself. Inviting educational leaders use open-ended questions to call forth investing behaviours. Brainstorming and participating in meaningful enquiry are also ways to promote investing. The ability to take enjoyment in going below the surface, to look at things in unique ways, to go off the beaten path, are manifestations of an investing spirit. In a pluralistic democratic society, investing can be a means to extend the moral imagination necessary to develop creative approaches to change. The problems of the present require more than the solutions of the past.

Coping

Coping deals with the ability to meet expectations and not to be overwhelmed. With escalating and often contradictory expectations coming at students, teachers and administrators from all angles, it is becoming more and more difficult to satisfy everyone. Inviting educational leaders can assist people in coping by giving a perspective on the past, clarity about the present and hope for the future. The ability to use ideals as guides and not millstones is vital in promoting coping behaviours. Similarly, being able prudently to use standards and test results as means to understand what is happening and what you might do to make things better are indicators of a sound educational perspective. Coping is promoted when you take a long-range perspective and see mistakes as feedback on the way to improvement. In order to do better, you must first do. Inviting educational leaders possess the savvy and determination to continue to move forward as they meet the prevailing educational winds, rather than being blown over by the periodic gust of hot and cold air.

Artfully orchestrating these four areas through imaginative acts of hope enables people to develop the desire and disposition to become life-long learners. To discover that you can learn important things and that you want to continue learning are the greatest educational discoveries. It enables mindful learning to flourish.

Mindful learning

John Dewey (1938) used the concepts of continuity and interaction to describe the perceptions we bring to any situation and the new perceptions that emerge. We need both sets of perceptions. To be too rigid about what we bring with us is to miss the present and its new possibilities. To bring nothing with us to an encounter is to be so open-minded that nothing registers. The orchestrating of continuity and interaction can lead to mindful learning.

Mindful learning, as described by Ellen Langer (1989; 1997), focuses on using our previous perceptions as a springboard to new perceptions rather than as a dungeon of repetitious past perceptions. This mindful learning is characterised by the construction of new categories to understand something better, an openness to novelty and new information, an awareness of more than one perspective and an orientation to the present (1997: 23). Langer contrasts this with mindlessness – digging a deep perceptual rut by being on automatic pilot for extended periods.

Perhaps Langer overstates the case, but she does make points that those interested in invitational teaching and learning need to consider. Educating for mindfulness is vitally connected with promoting a positive self-concept as learner. It takes a strong belief in one's authentic learning capacity to avoid a 'hardening of the categories', to seek out information that will disturb one's previous mindset, and to take delight in finding other ways to look at events. Being mindful of some taken-for-granted things that get in the way of important learning should encourage educational leaders to examine such questionable practices as overlearning the basics, focusing on only one thing at a time, delaying gratification, emphasising rote memorisation and emphasising the 'right answer'. From the perceptual approach, these practices can constrict rather than expand a person's perceptual field. For example:

- *Practice makes perfect.* Learning only one way to do things and ignoring the context of application leads to mechanical repetition.
- *Be still and focus only on the matter at hand.* Creative distraction enables someone to find novelty to extend perceptions.
- *Delayed gratification is important.* Being able to find enjoyment in the ongoing process of learning keeps interest alive.
- *Rote memory is to be emphasised.* Without personal meaning and understanding, ideas are like Teflon – guaranteed not to stick.
- *It is valuable to remember everything.* Memory can get in the way of a fresh vantage point needed to actively process a new situation.

Whatever else a school should be, it should not be a place that constricts people's perceptual field. Perhaps this is what is referred to in the lyrics, 'We don't want no education. We don't want no thought control.' Being another brick in the wall is not conducive to leading a vibrant and fulfilling life. Depth of perception is enhanced as we mindfully encounter subjects that matter.

Valuing knowledge/knowing values

Education must continue to confront truth (falsity), beauty (ugliness), and goodness (evil), in full awareness of the problematic facets of these categories and the disagreements across cultures and subcultures. These concerns may be ancient, but they must be perennially revisited and refashioned. And the academic disciplines remain the best way to pursue this mission.

(Gardner, 1999: 35)

Perhaps Howard Gardner overstates the case. However, educators need to attend to the point he is making because of the tendency either to disregard or narrowly regard disciplinary learning.

Inviting educational leaders promote the savouring, understanding and bettering of individual and social experiences. This can be done in many ways, but is not to be done primarily in a haphazard, unstructured way. Howard Gardner (1999) provides a way to think more deeply about savouring, understanding and bettering as educational virtues. A virtue, as used here, means the steadfast pursuit of something worthwhile in the face of temptation. For example, Schrag (1988) suggests that rather than think of thinking as a skill, we should think of thoughtfulness as a virtue. A person practising the virtue of thoughtfulness would find ways to overcome the inclinations of impulsivity and rigidity. A way to remember this sense of virtue is to reflect on the words of Oscar Wilde who acclaimed his questionable virtue by noting that he could withstand anything, except temptation. Let's look at the three educational virtues promoted by inviting educational leaders and their connection to Gardner's work.

Savouring educational experiences

Savouring deals with the ability to seek, take in and appreciate more and more of our experiences with the world. The ability to create 'flow' experiences is one manifestation of this virtue. Flow is the ability to create challenging but not overwhelming opportunities. The virtuous practices needed in pursuing flow are the ability to focus, avoid non-productive distraction and develop the appropriate skills. Savouring can also come from enjoying the world around you. Dianne Ackerman (1990; 1999) shows how we can savour such things as smells, touch, taste, being outside or playing with our pets. Aldous Huxley (1989) suggests that people feel their appreciation for a meal by holding their first bite of food in their mouth for one minute and allowing their palates to take in the subtleties of what they would normally quickly swallow.

Gardner adds to an understanding of savouring by showing that it can also be pursued through an encounter with great works of beauty, such as the music of Mozart. This savouring of Mozart is not merely a good feeling about his work but also a deep sense of how a piece of art fits together and takes us beyond typical perceptions. It takes time and practice to be able to savour complex works of art. The virtue in this pursuit is to put ourselves in a position where we can appreciate a work of art and then let the encounter make its mark on us. This involves cognition, affect and will, coming together in significant learning.

Understanding disciplinary knowledge

To understand is to grasp the meaning or reasonableness of something. It can be differentiated from mere rote learning in which you can say the right words in the right order but the meaningfulness of what is said is lacking. Recently, I visited a school and talked with a student who was studying for a test. He had a long list of words he was memorising. I asked him if he understood the words, and he told me he tried that once but that resulted in a lower test score. He had learned that understanding takes time and gets in the way of remembering all the facts you need to have in your mind to get marks. This showed me that the testing system was getting in the way of understanding and was anti-educational.

Gardner's contention is that educators should teach for deep under-standing by focusing on a few key disciplinary ideas and exploring them in depth. He gives, as an example, studying an aspect of evolution to understand the intricacies of its working. His point is 'to give students access to the "intellectual heart" or "experiential soul" of a discipline' (1999: 157). Taking this point of view to heart, inviting educational leaders should point out that if we wish students to understand more important ideas, we should teach less material, but what we teach should be taught in much more depth. The job of educators is not to cover, but to uncover material. This is done by starting with students' present perceptions and connecting them to the logic and understanding of disciplinary experts. Time and expertise are needed to take students beyond the intuitions of their unschooled minds (Gardner, 1991), to get beyond their misconceptions, their rote algorithms and their stereotypes of people and situations. This requires intellectually interested and interesting educators who embody rich understanding and the spirit of enquiry themselves.

Bettering human experience

Because we have a sense of better or worse in our experiences, we can engage in ethical thinking about the nature of good and evil. Inviting educational leaders do not believe that good things will automatically come about or bad things cannot change. They understand that through judicious and sustained imaginative acts of hope, there is the possibility of good things being made better or bad things being made less bad. This virtue of meliorism can be applied to any aspect of their personal or professional life. The temptation in ethical thinking is to give in to pessimism, to the idea that there is nothing that can be done to stop the negative from advancing. This is an important issue for students to consider. Gardner provides the example of students studying the holocaust to examine to what extent this horrific act of systematic genocide was planned well in advance or emerged from a set of circumstances. His point is that as students examine an aspect of evil, they come to a deeper understanding of the complexity of human behaviour and a subtle understanding of the banality of evil. The study of meaningful issues with substantive content invites depth of thought, feeling and the resolve necessary to come to grips with difficult moral issues.

The significance of Gardner's insights to the inviting perspective is to point out the difference between the world *of* knowledge and the world *for* knowledge. The world of knowledge represents the academic disciplines – the structured, cumulative, critical study of an aspect of experience. The world for knowledge stands for the world at large that is open for experience and can be examined. To emphasise only one of these is to be limited and out of touch with deeper possibilities. Studying key concepts in the academic disciplines can give depth of thought, feeling and purpose. An openness and examination of the world around can provide relevance, surprise and adventure. Connecting the world of and for knowledge can invite a deep vitality and a vital depth. In a world that is often tempting us to be superficial consumers of more and more questionable 'goods', these are not bad virtues to possess.

From a perceptual point of view, thinking and feeling are fundamentally connected. In our intellectual goals for schools we do not have to choose between neurotic know-it-alls and contented know-nothings. Although thoughts without feeling are empty, feelings without thoughts are blind. There is a need to orchestrate artfully the two. To this end, inviting educational leadership is about creating schools that promote the development of a healthy self-concept-as-learner, a vibrant mindfulness in learning, and a deepening desire and capacity to understand and connect the world of knowledge and the world for knowledge.

Summary

- People with good self-concepts-as-learners can relate, assert, invest and cope well.
- Mindful learning uses previous learning as a springboard for new learning.
- Mindful learning means often getting beyond educational bromides.
- Regarding thinking as a virtue means moving beyond formulae.
- Savouring is about being able to appreciate the uniqueness of particulars.
- Disciplined understanding requires the virtue of thinking and the rewards of savouring.
- A deeper understanding of the world *of* knowledge can lead to more mindful exploration of the world *for* knowledge.
- An openness to the world *for* knowledge can lead to a deeper exploration of the world *of* knowledge.

Extending the conversation

Q: Is it enough for students to feel good about themselves?

A: Self-concept-as-learner is a part of all learning but it is not all there is to learning. It can serve as a good base for present and future learning. If we ignore self-concept-as-learner we miss an important ingredient needed for self-directed learning.

Q: Students and teachers may be relating all the time in school. Can't there be too much relating?

A: Of course not all relating is productive. Students and others in schools need to stress educational relating. This is relating that enables people to question each other, give reasons for what they think and develop any questions they may have.

Q: Isn't learning delayed gratification important for becoming an adult?

A: Learning to delay external rewards can certainly be important. However, learning to delay the reward of understanding what is being done or the meaningfulness of present learning is not positive. We don't learn because something is hard but because it is worthwhile.

Q: If thinking is a virtue, are children doing something wrong if they are not practising this virtue?

A: Only you would think of a question like this. Thinking of thinking as a virtue emphasises the personal effort that is needed to practise good thinking. However, good thinking also involves background knowledge and a positive feeling about the meaningfulness of what is to be studied. Children who are learning to think better are not doing something wrong if they are not practising good thinking in the present. However, adults – who should know better – are lacking virtue if they refuse to think deeply about important issues.

Q: Is savouring really all that important?

A: Learning to appreciate something requires effort, patience and honesty. To take this habit into all we do can provide people with a deeper sense of meaningfulness and possibility.

Q: Isn't disciplined understanding too difficult for too many students?

A: Without understanding, much of the curriculum is like Teflon – guaranteed not to stick. Disciplined understanding can help students get at the roots of enquiry and develop the habits of going below the surface. In a democracy, this should not be the prerogative of only the few.

Q: Why emphasise the world of and for knowledge?

A: What is learned in school should connect to the world in not-textbook ways if it is going to make a difference. Since schools are about making a difference, texts should be used as mean to develop a deeper appreciation and understanding of the world outside school.

Q: How can anyone manage to learn all of this?

A: Ah, you are already anticipating the next chapter. Time to move on.

References

Ackerman, D.A. (1990) *A Natural History of the Senses*. New York: Random House.

Ackerman, D.A. (1999) *Deep Play*. New York: Random House.

Dewey, J. (1938) *Experience and Education*. New York: Macmillan.

Finger, J. (1995) 'A Study of Professional and Inferred Self-Concept-as-Learner of Male African American Middle Grade Students'. Unpublished doctoral dissertation. University of North Carolina, Greensboro.

Gardner, H. (1991) *The Unschooled Mind: How Children Think and How Schools Should Teach*. New York: BasicBooks.

Gardner, H. (1999) *The Disciplined Mind: What All Students Should Understand*. New York: Simon and Schuster.

Harper, K.L. and Purkey, W.W. (1993) 'Self-concept-as-learner of middle level students', *Research in Middle Level Education* 17 (1), 79–89.

Huxley, A. (1989) *Island*. Toronto: Harper Canada.

Langer, E. (1989) *Mindfulness*. Reading, MA: Addison-Wesley.

Langer, E. (1997) *The Power of Mindful Learning*. Reading, MA: Addison-Wesley.

Purkey, W.W., Cage, B. and Graves, W.H. (1973) 'The Florida Key: a scale to infer learner self-concept', *Journal of Educational and Psychological Measurement*, 33, 979–84.

Schrag, F. (1988) *Thinking in School and Society*. New York: Routledge.

Seligman, M. (1991) *Learned Optimism*. New York: Knopf.

8
■ ■ ■

Managing
Thoughtfulness

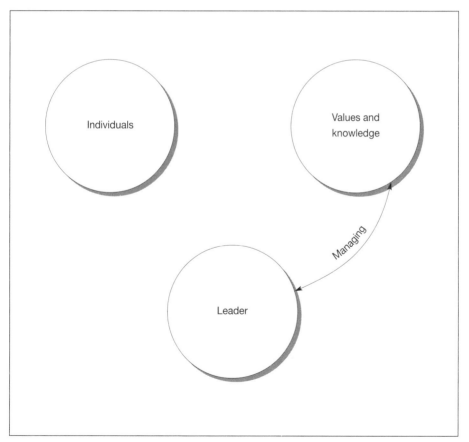

Figure 8.1: Managing thoughtfulness

Inviting educational leaders think about caring and care about thinking. By cultivating an ethic of care and thoughtfulness they are able to extend basic principles of invitational learning, promote successful intelligence and develop ethical fitness.

What is an ethic of care?

Are there some basic principles of learning?

Can we cultivate the practice of successful intelligence?

What does it mean to be ethically fit?

Because of the care necessary to promote thoughtfulness, these are questions that need to be asked as educational leaders manage meaningful learning for themselves and others. This chapter is *unlikely* to connect with your beliefs if you:

- don't care about caring;
- don't like to think about thinking;
- think that learning to think better is only an individual issue;
- think ethics is fundamentally about following strict rules.

This chapter is more *likely* to connect with your beliefs if you:

- think caring is vital for learning;
- feel that learning centres around personal and societal meanings;
- believe that thinking about thinking is important;
- think ethics is about judicious and caring judgement.

Just as students send the message to teachers that, 'We don't care what you know until we know that you care', teachers are often sending that same message to their colleagues and supervisors. Perhaps, to paraphrase an old song, when it comes to working in schools, people seem to be saying, 'I won't learn my share, if you don't show me care'. If we want people to engage in mindful learning, we have to operate from a caring core.

Working from a caring core

The need for care in our present culture is acute. Patients feel uncared for in our medical system; clients feel uncared for in our welfare system; old people feel uncared for in the facilities provided for them; and children, especially adolescents, feel uncared for in schools.

(Noddings, 1992: xi)

Perhaps Nel Noddings overstates her case. However, the point most people would agree with is that person-intensive educational endeavours are unable to sustain themselves without a caring core. This is especially true in developing approaches to thoughtfulness.

Inviting educational leadership works from a stance with caring at the core. This caring stance is not so much about managing care as it is about managing to care in ways that communicate trust, intentionality, respect and optimism. This is very difficult now, as Noddings observed, because there are more and more challenges to caring in schools. A seemingly never-ending list of pressures make it difficult to care – large classes, a curriculum disassociated from student's interests, pressure to get high test scores, negative feelings against educators from those outside schools, educators' negative feelings against those who are castigating them, and the list can go on. Notwithstanding all these difficulties, education is fundamentally a caring profession. Without care, educational leaders are just going through the motions and much positive learning of anything of importance will have difficulty taking hold.

If educators care that students become thoughtful learners, students need to learn that educators care both about them and good thinking. This is more likely to happen if educators use the four major components of Noddings's ethic of caring to provide a solid interpersonal connection (1992: 22–5). These four components are modelling, dialogue, practice and confirmation. Each of these components needs further elaboration:

- *Modelling*. Caring is not about telling people we care but about establishing caring relationships with them. Similarly, teaching for thoughtfulness is not about telling people to be thoughtful. It is enhanced as we show people how and why we think about an issue that has mutual meaning. Applied to inviting educational leadership, this means that educators should be able to give an educational reason for anything they are doing in schools.

- *Dialogue*. By engaging in open-ended conversations in which there is a mutual search for understanding, all involved can learn more about the topic, each other and themselves. This enables people to develop deeper relationships with each other, and the process of trying to sort out the world more meaningfully is seen as a shared human endeavour rather than a lonely, frightening chore. Asking honest, open-ended questions is a way to mutually explore issues of meaning.

- *Practice.* Caring is not merely to be talked about, it is to be put into action. Schools need real caring projects in which all involved are invited to participate. Talking about issues that come up in these projects and trying to put some new suggestions into practice deepen the thinking about caring and the caring about thinking.
- *Confirmation.* In a caring relationship the care-giver needs to be rooted in a hopefulness that the other person's better self is there waiting to be called forth. This calling forth is done not by formula but through imaginative acts of hope that can be examined and improved by self-correcting enquiry. Confirmation is about making and sustaining a live connection with the other.

Working from a caring core is not a technique that an educator puts into practice, but a virtue he or she embodies. Virtues, as Rebore (2001: 28, 30) has noted, include a number of characteristics. They:

- shape a person's very core;
- are adapted to the situations a person is in;
- dispose people to act in certain ways;
- integrate emotional and intellectual life;
- need to be cultivated over time to grow.

The management of the virtue of educational caring is about artfully orchestrating feelings, thoughts and actions to develop deeper and broader possibilities for meaning. This virtue can grow as it is fused with an invitational interpretation of basic principles of learning.

Invitational learning

Inviting educational leaders seek to create a total school environment where people want to be and want to learn meaningful and important things. These leaders care about learning in which people actualise more of their individual, cognitive, emotional, physical and social potential and contribute to the democratic development of their community and the larger global society. Ronald Brandt (1998: 15), summarising research on learning, notes ten guidelines he feels educators need to reflect on, elaborate and apply, to make them personally meaningful. Examined from the point of view of invitational leadership and the virtue of educational caring, these guidelines provide some help in managing the learning that is necessary to develop thoughtfulness. The interpreted principles are as follows:

1 *People learn what is personally meaningful to them.* From the point of view of self-concept theory, people attend more to whatever is closest to the centre of self. The roles and attributes that people value now and in some perceived future self provide a link between what they would like to learn and what needs to be taught. We ignore a person's meaning structure at our own peril. Teachers and leaders need to be able to act as translators who can connect what people want to learn with what they have to teach. They are able to connect the psychology of the person to the logic of the subject they are teaching and in the process the perceptual fields of both the teacher and the learner are extended.

2 *People learn when they accept challenging but achievable goals.* Nobody really wants to be overwhelmed or underwhelmed for any long period of time. Anxiety and boredom take their toll on human potential. Finding the right whelm level and then providing coaching and personally meaningful materials so that people can make progress on a meaningful and challenging goal enables important learning to take place. Moving toward the goal of enabling people to do this for themselves is what being an autotelic learner is all about. Learning to learn is fuelled by the habit of learning to care about what you are doing while you are doing it.

3 *Learning is developmental.* Although no two perceptual fields and no two self-concepts are the same, people can go through similar stages and face similar learning needs for structure, content and meaning. Educators need to develop pedagogical materials and leading styles that enable them to move to greater or lesser degrees of complexity as necessary for the person and situation. It is important not to get locked into a narrow view of development and think that people can only exhibit behaviour from one stage. A leader operating from a caring perspective sees the person and not the stage. A leader's openness to the other person, and a flexibility and fluency in dealing with ideas and concepts, are essential to call forth unique learning potential.

4 *People learn well when they can learn in their own way and have some degree of choice and control.* Invitational education's emphasis on respect for the person and its link to the democratic ethos support this principle. Each person has a unique perceptual field, with meanings and insights that have to be taken into consideration. When we can understand the 'psychologic' of the other person, we can think with him or her about designing learning opportunities. When we create shared perceptions, we can both expand our perceptual fields.

5 *People learn well when they use what they already know as they construct new knowledge.* People are not blank slates. They work within their personal world of meaning to understand what is happening. Each person builds on previous perceptions to develop working hypotheses that fit what they think will be happening in the future. By developing the habit of imaginatively experimenting with, and adding to, one's perceptual field in a thoughtful way, each person is what can be called a personal scientist (Kelly, 1963).

6 *People learn well when they have opportunities for social interaction.* Sharing perceptions with others enables a person to articulate, clarify and extend what may previously have been vague. A person may not know what he or she thinks until after he or she begins talking. Participating in a group that asks for clarity or further elaboration of perceptions can help a person to develop new ways to express and experience more complex thoughts and arguments.

7 *People learn well when they get helpful feedback.* Feedback is the basis for self-correcting enquiry. It enables us to make the necessary changes to solve a problem or fashion a product. A helpful strategy for educators employing specific feedback is to tell the recipient what they did well, what needs improvement and how they might go about making the change. The gentle art of illuminating strengths and weaknesses of present behaviour can be the most subtle teaching–learning strategy to learn.

8 *People learn well when they acquire and use strategies.* Strategies can give people a way to begin and a feel for logic to follow. It is important that strategies do not become straightjackets or mindless algorithms. To become mindful, people using a learning strategy need to become aware of different contexts and variations that need to be made to their learning strategy. This is one of the reasons why disciplinary understanding is important. It can be a vital source of more complex and imaginative strategies of enquiry.

9 *People learn well when they experience a positive emotional climate.* Invitational learning is about the orchestration of people, places, policies, programmes and processes to call forth human potential. Nothing in the school setting is neutral. All learning environments can be intentionally arranged. Feeling safe and yet challenged enables a person to explore and expand perceptions, rather than defend oneself from distractions and threat. Being a part of a community of learners is a way for there to be continued social support for learning.

10 *People learn well when the learning environment supports the intended learning.* Not only should the environment be positive, it should also be specific in the ways it helps people solve problems. This can include having maps, charts, diagrams and learning groups available so that intelligence can be well distributed throughout the environment (Perkins, 1992: 152).

Applying these principles enables educational leaders to attend to *what* is learned (that which is personally meaningful, challenging and developmentally appropriate); *how* it is learned (building on choice, previous knowledge, interaction, feedback and strengths); and *where* it is learned (in positive and supportive environments). Using these basic principles to focus effort is an important step in managing learning and intellectual life. This management process can be further directed to focus on the insights of successful intelligence.

Managing successful intelligence

It is my contention that successful intelligence should be taught, because it is the kind of intelligence that will be the most valuable and rewarding in the real world after school – both in our work and our personal lives.

(Sternberg 1996: 269)

Robert Sternberg believes that educational leaders must develop a perspective on intelligence that they can embody and promote in schools. If it is important to learn that you can learn throughout your life, then Sternberg's successful intelligence is a good perspective to consider because it looks beyond the narrow confines of school to life issues with which everyone has to deal. For example, I have a friend who has been unsuccessful in more things than anyone I know. My friend has also been successful in more things than anyone I know. My friend's motto is, 'If you want to succeed in many things, you have to try many more things'. My friend is an exemplar of Sternberg's successful intelligence.

Successful intelligence is 'the kind of intelligence that matters to everyone in reaching important goals' (Sternberg, 1996: 13). It is a blending of creative, analytic and practical thinking used to achieve a goal. This blending involves finding good problems to pursue and good initial solutions to those problems, and then making those good solutions even better. Looking at successful intelligence from the inside out, it is the process of calling forth self-activation rather than self-sabotage. Learning how to use successful intelligence in our own life is a way to invite ourselves both personally and professionally.

Here are some characteristics that Sternberg has found in successfully intelligent people (pp. 251–9):

- *They know how to make the most out of their abilities.* By exploring many options, they discover what they do well and build on their strengths. They find ways to compensate for their shortcomings.
- *They translate thought into action.* Rather than getting buried in the 'paralysis of analysis', they find ways to act on their ideas. Ideas are seen as hypotheses to be ventured forth.
- *They are not afraid to risk failure.* As Sternberg notes, 'Successfully intelligent people make mistakes, but not the same mistake twice'. To fail to learn something from a mistake is the mistake to avoid (p. 262).
- *They have the ability to concentrate on the big picture.* By not getting bogged down by details, they can put their energy into what matters in getting a problem solved. By having a sense of where they want to go, they can take better means of transportation.
- *They have a reasonable level of self-confidence.* They are not too intimidated or too bold in their undertakings. They are not filled with self-doubts or self-delusions, for both of these are unreal starting points for significant actions.

These are just six of the 20 characteristics listed by Sternberg about people who have become accomplished achievers. More detailed explorations of this approach can be found in the later book by Sternberg and Grigorenko (2000).

Managing for educational thoughtfulness is embedded in an ethic of care, sound principles of learning and successful intelligence. It is extended as educational leaders work to become ethically fit.

Developing ethical fitness

We will not survive the morality of repetition: The twenty-first century's choices are simply too tough. Nor will we survive the morality of relativism: There is too much leverage these days behind even a single unpunished act of evil. We'll survive by a morality of mindfulness. We'll survive where reason moderates the clash of values and intuition schools our decision making. There's no better way for good people to make tough choices.

(Kidder, 1996: 222)

The point Rushmore Kidder makes is that managing thoughtfulness needs to include concrete guidelines and principles for handling the difficult ethical issues we face in everyday life. It is not enough for inviting leaders to be thoughtful. It is also necessary to apply care, good thinking and firm resolve to ethical dilemmas and issues involving conflicting goods.

According to Kidder, thoughtfulness is not usually extended as we face right-versus-wrong choices. If we have a choice between what is made up of the good, the true and the beautiful and what is heavily laden with the bad, the false and the ugly, then we do not have a dilemma. We merely need the resolve to do what we think is right and do it. Thoughtfulness, however, is extended as we face right-versus-right issues. These are ethical dilemmas in which there is a tension between these patterns of contesting rights:

- *Truth versus loyalty*: you have to decide between straightforward honesty or promoting your school's reputation.
- *Individual versus community*: an unruly student who will gain from being in a regular classroom makes it difficult for others to learn.
- *Short-term versus long-term*: you can improve immediate test scores but students will probably retain a strong distaste for the subject.
- *Justice versus mercy*: a student who is making much improvement violates a zero-tolerance directive.

These issues are moral dilemmas in which we may often have half a mind going one way and the other half going the other way. We have to decide, often in a split second, and we cannot go both ways. Kidder suggests that these agonising issues will not go away and what we need to develop is ethical fitness.

Ethical fitness is 'a capacity to recognize the nature of moral challenges and respond with a well-tuned conscience, a lively perception of the difference between right and wrong, and an ability to choose the right and live by it' (Kidder, 1996: 56). Building on the perceptual tradition's emphasis on making distinctions that make a difference, developing ethical fitness depends on differentiating right from wrong and right from right. This involves being mentally engaged in examining real issues on a regular basis and being committed to act on your best judgement in each case (p. 59). In order to assist with the development of ethical fitness, Kidder suggests that the following nine steps be followed (pp. 183–6):

1 *Recognise that there is a moral issue.* Is this an issue that involves a right-versus-wrong or a right-versus-right perspective?

2 *Determine the actor.* To what extent and in what ways am I responsible for what is happening in the present and the future?

3 *Gather the relevant facts.* What details do I need to know to find out what is happening?

4 *Test for right-versus-wrong issues.* Does this involve a fundamental violation of principles, terrible consequences or a total lack of care?

5 *Test for right-versus-right paradigms.* Which two deeply held values are in conflict with one another?

6 *Apply the resolution principles.* How does being aware of my duties, the consequences of what is happening and my desire to extend care in this situation influence what I think is possible and desirable?

7 *Investigate the 'trilemma' options.* Can I imagine going beyond the either/or possibilities I am faced with?

8 *Make the decision.* How can I summon up the moral courage to act on what my reflected judgement has shown to be the right thing to do?

9 *Revisit and reflect on the decision.* What have I learned in taking action on this decision?

Developing the virtues of ethical fitness is not easy or without its costs. It takes time and some degree of agonising to become a more thoughtful human being. Kidder's nine-step process is not, as he admits, a panacea. It does, however, present an heuristic for assisting invitational leaders in managing an important aspect of thoughtfulness – one that many educators hope would just go away. As an educational perspective aimed at calling forth human potential, the inviting approach has to face and grow from such encounters. Such growth is more possible in inviting educational communities, which is the topic of the next chapter.

Summary

- Working from a caring core is demonstrated in modelling, dialogue, practice and confirmation.
- Invitational learning is manifested in what is learned, how it is learned and when it is learned.
- Successful intelligence is a blend of creative, analytical and practical thinking, used to reach a goal.
- Achievers of successful intelligence have a reasonable level of self-esteem.
- Ethical fitness is developed by attending to right-versus-right value issues.
- Ethical thinking involves judicious use of reasoning and intuition.
- Ethical thinking means dealing with the desire to care, along with attending to duties and consequences of actions.

Extending the conversation

Q: Doesn't the inviting approach mention caring too much?

A: Caring is at the core of inviting educational leadership. If you do not care, why would you want to do this. Because caring is a complex virtue, it needs to be examined in a variety of ways.

Q: How can invitational learning work when there are too many students in the class?

A: Invitational learning is based on a set of principles about how people can deal more meaningfully with the world of and for knowledge. These principles can be used to design lessons, to get students to work with one another and to develop portfolios, among other things. These principles are not dependent on how many students are in a class.

Q: Is successful intelligence just a pop psychology fad?

A: Robert Sternberg, the developer of successful intelligence, is IBM Professor of Psychology and Education at Yale University. His ideas are based on solid research. Interestingly, he mentioned that he became interested in successful intelligence because he was a poor test taker.

Q: What does it mean to have reasonable self-confidence?

A: Reasonable self-confidence means that a person can honestly examine his or her strengths and weaknesses and use this knowledge to reach goals. Diminishing or exaggerating one's abilities make it more difficult to reach many goals.

Q: Is ethical fitness something that should be developed in a gym?

A: Ethical fitness is a metaphorical way of saying that ethical thinking must be put into practice to improve. Merely thinking about ethical issues is not enough. Neither is taking a stand and acting on it without regard for the ethical complexities embedded in it. Ethical fitness means developing the habits of thoughtfulness and persistently applying them to reconciling value dilemmas.

Q: Does ethical thinking have to be agonising?

A: Ethical thinking does not have to be agonising. As a practice it has its own rewards and excellences that can be enjoyed. However, if honestly and persistently pursued, ethical thinking can be arduous. Sometimes that is the price we have to pay to live consciously and conscientiously.

Q: Does trying to become ethically fit have to be a lonely pursuit?

A: Becoming ethically fit is much easier if it is practised in an educational community. And, that is the topic for the next chapter.

References

Brandt, R. (1998) *Powerful Learning*. Alexandria, VA: Association for Supervision and Curriculum Development.

Kelly, G.A. (1963) *A Theory of Personality: The Psychology of Personal Constructs*. New York: W.W. Norton.

Kidder, R. (1996) *How Good People Make Tough Choices: Resolving the Dilemmas of Ethical Living*. New York: Fireside.

Noddings, N. (1992) *The Challenge to Care in School: An Alternative Approach to Education*. New York: Teachers College Press.

Perkins, D. (1992) *Smart Schools: From Training Memories to Educating Minds*. New York: Free Press.

Rebore, R.W. (2001) *The Ethics of Educational Leadership*. Upper Saddle River, NJ: Merrill Prentice Hall.

Sternberg, R.J. (1996) *Successful Intelligence: How Practical and Creative Intelligence Determine Success in Life*. New York: Simon Schuster.

Sternberg, R.J. and Grigorenko, E.L. (2000) *Teaching for Successful Intelligence: To Increase Student Learning and Achievement*. Arlington Heights, IL: Skylight.

9
■ ■ ■

Leading Educational Communities

Inviting educational leaders use figurative language to help structure a group's attention and put creative life into their activities. By viewing the school as an inviting family rather than an efficient factory, people, places, programmes, policies and processes can be directed to help develop humans' resources.

Is efficiency the most important goal for schools?

Is there one right way to structure a school?

How much structure do schools need?

How much freedom do schools need?

Because of the co-operation needed to make inviting schools work, these are questions that educational leaders need to ask as they work with people to make educational communities. This chapter is *unlikely* to connect with your beliefs if you:

● think that efficiency is the most important goal of schools;

● believe there is only one way to structure a school;

● feel that schools do not need any structures;

● think that freedom is merely the absence of constraints.

This chapter is more *likely* to connect with your beliefs if you:

● think that co-operation is a vital goal for schools;

● believe there are many principled ways to structure a good school;

118

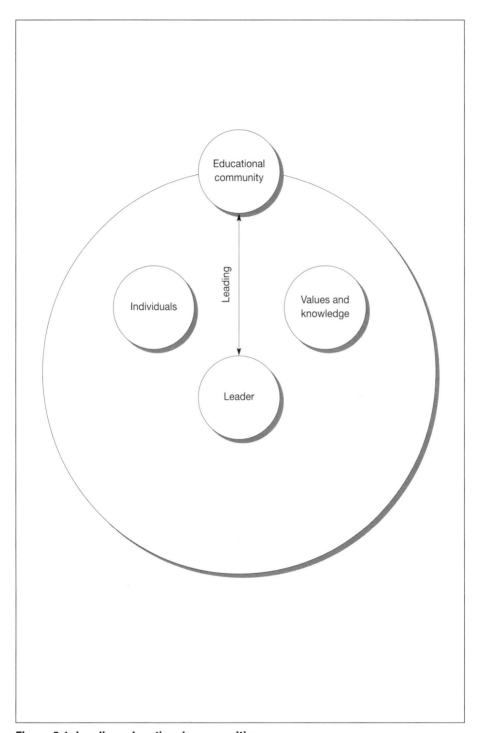

Figure 9.1: Leading educational communities

- feel that a thoughtful structure can encourage freedom;
- can see freedom as the ability to do meaningful things.

Robert Pirsig (1992) asks the question, 'How do atoms become chemistry professors?' In answering this unusual question he presents a theory of how energy moves from the physical, to the biological, to the social and finally to the intellectual by means of what he calls structure and freedom. Structure, for Pirsig, is what protects emerging processes and gives them a chance to take hold. Freedom refers to the new, more complex interactions that develop as a result of the protection provided by the structure. This freedom brings new possibilities for more complex patterns of interaction to develop. Structure without freedom would be mere repetition and nothing new would emerge. Freedom without structure could not sustain itself, and nothing new could come into existence. New qualities emerge as structure and freedom work together.

Over aeons and aeons, this conjoining of structure and freedom enabled energy to move from operating within the laws of nature (the physical level of mechanical interaction), to the 'law of the jungle' (the biological level, which necessitates the importance of survival and reproduction), to 'the law' (the social level where humans can encode rules), and finally to the law of the dialectic (the intellectual level where human beings can develop more complex understandings of how each of the previous levels works and, eventually, to where chemistry professors can understand atoms). Likewise, the growth of complexity in all forms of organisational life needs both freedom and structure to avoid ruts and provide protection for creativity and intellectually deeper forms of interaction to take hold and flourish. It is the job of inviting educational leaders to help develop structures that enable more thoughtful forms of learning and connection to take hold.

Inviting educational leadership can be viewed as providing and sustaining structures for imaginative acts of hope to take hold. One structure for these imaginative acts of hope are compelling images. Inviting leaders think about the images they use and direct their thinking towards images that can call forth the power of people, places, policies, programmes and processes to work towards a common valued end. In working towards a common valued end, people have to communicate, and in the process of communication they form communities (Dewey, 1916). This chapter looks at schools in terms of the image of inviting families and seeks to harmonise their structure and freedom with this in mind.

The inviting family school model

Structure and freedom are important in the running of schools. If the structure is too rigid or too tight, the opportunity for creative interaction to develop is lessened. On the other hand, if freedom occurs without any protection, anything goes and nothing takes hold. What is needed is a judicious balance of structure and freedom so that educational forms of caring, thinking and doing are maintained, protected and enhanced.

Schools in a pluralistic, democratic society need both freedom and structure to function humanely. Schools need freedom – the ability to do things in different ways – because there is no one, preconceived and final set of procedures to deal with the unique factors that any particular school faces. There is a need for experimentation, diversity and change. Schools need structure because some pattern of organisation is necessary to make sure that the essential functions are handled. There is a need for a sound, humane and imaginative way to do things. Let's look at two images that are competing for the heart of education – the efficient factory school and the inviting family school.

The efficient factory school

Although factories are changing, their traditional form of organisation lives on in the minds, hearts and practices in the schools of many. Factories, to make money, have to be efficient. Interestingly, this efficiency, if narrowly defined, can get in the way of making money in the long run. Narrowly defined efficiency results in the following six characteristics: mass production, uniform product, cost effectiveness, technology, centralised control and workers as functionaries (Purkey and Novak, 1996). Applied to schools, these characteristics can be portrayed as follows:

- *Mass production*. There is an emphasis on bigger schools with more and more students taking a narrowly prescribed curriculum in a lock-step, automatic way. Choice is minimised.
- *Uniform product*. Students are expected to meet performance indicators that are measured by standardised test scores. Those who are out of step can be sent to the equivilent of a factory-outlet store for standardised remediation.
- *Cost effectiveness*. With the pressure on getting a 'bigger bang for the budgeted buck', aesthetic concerns are minimised and programmes that do not provide immediate payback in terms of standardised test scores are eliminated.

- *Technology*. The school is dominated by machines and high status is attained by having the latest equipment. Students and staff are expected to be up to speed and to fit the machines.
- *Centralised control*. Central headquarters mandates what is to be done and a wider gap develops between the mandator and the mandated. Hierarchical professional relationships dominate the organisation.
- *Workers as functionaries*. Teachers, staff and students are continually told what to do. Teachers are seen as expendable and interchangeable and expected to comply with orders.

The inviting family school

This factory image of schools can be compared to the image of the school as an inviting family. This alternative image is presented because much of the heart of education will be severed if educators are seen merely as functionaries and students as resources to be fit into a hyperactive economic system.

Just as schools in a democracy are varied, so too are inviting families. They can come in a variety of shapes and sizes and are not limited by traditional relationships. The structure that holds inviting families together is based on a commitment to a way of being with each other. This way of being with each other is characterised by the following six characteristics of the inviting family (Purkey and Novak, 1996; Novak, 1999; Novak and Purkey, 2001):

- *Respect for individual uniqueness*. Each member of the family is viewed as incomparable and can offer something that is appreciated by the other members. Members are given more choices in what they contribute to the family as they get older.
- *Co-operative spirit*. Family members have a sense that 'we are all in this together'. They care for and accept care from each other.
- *Sense of belonging*. Members spend time with one another and share a sense of loyalty and warmth for each other.
- *Pleasing habitat*. Emphasis is placed on making the residence alive with plants, colour and comfort.
- *Positive expectations*. Family members are appreciated in the present and are encouraged to develop their unique talents and fulfil their responsibilities.

- *Vital connections to society*. Family members take their interests and talents out to the world and share and deliberate what they have encountered with others in the family.

Taking seriously each of these characteristics, the following checklist has been developed (Novak, 1999), and can be of use in examining a school in terms of its relationship to an inviting family:

1 *Respect for individual uniqueness*

   What is positive and unique about this school?

   Are evaluations made in a caring way?

   How are students and others offered assistance if they are having difficulties?

   How is uniqueness celebrated?

2 *Co-operative spirit*

   Is mutual support stressed over competition?

   How do people take co-operative responsibility?

   Do students, staff and parents have a say in making decisions?

   Is peer teaching encouraged?

3 *Sense of belonging*

   Is the school perceived as a caring place?

   Is there a core nurturing person for each student?

   How are people treated during and after absences?

   What shared social events are there in the school?

4 *Pleasing habitat*

   Does the school appear cared for?

   Who is involved in caring for the school?

   Are there green plants in the school?

   Does the school feel alive with positive things?

5 *Positive expectations*

   Can administrators say good things about each teacher?

   Can teachers say good things about each of their students?

   Can students say good things about their teachers and administrators?

   What are some imaginative acts of hope demonstrated in the school?

6 *Vital connections to society*

   How active is the school in the outside community?

How visible is the outside community in the school?

Are volunteers encouraged in the school?

To what extent are larger societal and global issues deliberated in the school?

These questions are meant to be discussion starters. If they seem strange or out of place, people may wish to reassess the image that guides the school. This inviting school image can also be used to examine the spirit in which the essential functions of the school are carried out.

Inviting the essentials

The inviting family model is an ideal that has come from people's everyday experience. It is hoped that many people can identify with the importance of good family experiences. Through critical and imaginative reflection on family experiences, an extended list of characteristics can be developed that can then be applied to education. The family model is also supported by research on people who are self-directed learners. Csikszentmihalyi (1990) cites research on how the family context can promote the development of autotelic people. He notes five factors:

1 *Clarity*: children know what is expected of them; they know the general direction in which they should be heading.

2 *Centring*: people are interested in what children are doing in the present; children are appreciated in their uniqueness.

3 *Choice*: children have a variety of possibilities; they are not locked into one way of being or one way to do things.

4 *Trust*: children feel unselfconscious in trying new things; they have been provided the structure to develop creative responses.

5 *Challenge*: parents provide complex opportunities for their children; children are participants in engaging activities.

This research connects with the inviting family model and the promotion of educational living. It also connects with research on educational leadership.

Turning to research on education, Reginald Green (2001: 65) found that in schools that were becoming learning organisations:

- teachers possessed in-depth knowledge of students' in-school and out-of-school lives;

- there existed a collective sense of caring and responsibility for student success;
- a sense of family existed in the school and there was a sense of collaboration among professionals.

It seems that schools researched by Green are working to improve their structures by moving to an inviting family model rather than an efficient factory model of schooling. This movement to an inviting family model can be directed to the essential functions of schools so that conventions based on inviting principles can be developed (Postman and Weingartner, 1973). Four principles can guide the development of inviting conventions:

1 *All people can learn*. Questions to consider: All children can learn what? What happens if they don't learn?
2 *All people want to learn*. Questions to consider: Want to learn what? How can we connect what they want to learn to what we have to teach?
3 *We can find ways to engage people in meaningful learning*. Questions to consider: How can we tell what is meaningful to different people? How can we work with people to construct meaningful activities?
4 *We can find ways to enjoy ourselves in the process*. Questions to consider: If we are not enjoying what we are doing, what are we doing wrong? If we are enjoying what we are doing, how can we keep doing it?

These are just a few of the questions that can be asked from an inviting perspective as schools examine their conventions. Although all inviting schools do not look alike and there are a multitude of conventions that can be created from an inviting perspective, it is important to have an inviting family model to help in developing the specifics. Returning to Postman and Weingartner's conventional functions (pp. 31–44), the following basic guidelines can be added:

- *Time structuring*: the school allows some flexibility in how time is used and students can make decisions in how to organise their own time.
- *Activity structuring*: students are actively involved in their learning, which takes place both within and outside the school.
- *Defining intelligence, worthwhile knowledge, good behaviour*: successful intelligence is stressed, along with knowledge that enables students to savour, understand and better more of their present and future experiences and meaningfully connect with the world of and for knowledge.

- *Evaluation*: the illumination of strengths and weaknesses enables students to achieve success in various challenging ways and is not to be primarily test-driven.
- *Supervision*: students can be involved in the governance of the school and in the directing of some of its activities.
- *Role differentiation*: all people in the school are potential educational leaders who are encouraged to use their experiences to bring about more responsible learning.
- *Accountability to the public*: community and parental participation is encouraged and the school is willing to be accountable for what it considers to be its educational mandate.
- *Accountability to the future*: the school aims to enable all who partici-pate in its operations to advance their desire and capacity to learn and their respect for evidential reasoning as they confront important present and future life issues.

With these guidelines in mind, invitational leaders can encourage the participation of all in the leadership of their educational community. This task is made easier with the specific inviting suggestions for man-aging people, places, policies, programmes and processes presented in the next chapter.

Summary

- All institutions require structure and freedom.
- Schools can be viewed as inviting families rather than efficient factories.
- Factory schools emphasise mass production and teachers as functionaries.
- Inviting family schools stress belonging, co-operation and positive expectations.
- Schools can be examined by using a checklist based on the inviting family model.
- Schools can structure their conventions around an inviting family model.

Extending the conversation

Q: Isn't it a bit of a stretch to go from atoms to chemistry professors to schools?

A: I see this as an imaginative attempt to connect abstract principles. Perhaps the better question is 'Does this give us a better understanding of how institutions work?' I think the tension between structure and freedom describes a lot that is happening in schools and other parts of life. If the idea fits, use it.

Q: Are you saying that cost efficiency is not important in education?

A: Certainly educators should not be wasteful. However, there are contexts in which the language of efficiency seems out of place. For example, it would seem unusual to ask if someone was an efficient friend. There is a different sensibility involved.

Q: Is the inviting school anti-technology?

A: Certainly the inviting school is not anti-technology. It does, however, want to place technology in the service of educational living. If technology means the study of the techniques, tools and artefacts we use, then the inviting school should be pro-technology. This type of study should help us better use these tools rather than being used by them.

Q: Isn't the inviting family school too idealistic for the world we live in today?

A: Ideals should be judged on whether they get us to do better things. Looking at schools as inviting families should enable us to make sure that care is ever present in the educational work we do. Since people come from families and have an idea of what a good family can do, this seems like a rich metaphor to use. Can you think of a better metaphor for emphasising care in schools?

Q: Aren't families sanctuaries from the indifference of the outside world?

A: Families do many things. Certainly they can make us stronger to face more of the world's challenges. However, as we bring more of the outside world into the family, the family can also become more complex.

Q: Isn't the checklist for the inviting family too mechanistic?

A: The checklist is a device for starting a conversation for improving a school. If it can call attention to areas that should be celebrated or changed, it has done its job.

Q: Why did you not give us specific conventions to put in our schools?

A: Beware of people who tell you exactly what to do in your school. People who are closest to the situation should have an important say in what is done and how it is done. This book provides a perspective for focusing and developing inviting conventions. That's an important beginning.

Q: How are we supposed to manage all these details?

A: Glad you asked. That's what we will look at in the next chapter.

References

Csikszentmihalyi, M. (1990) *Flow: The Psychology of Optimal Experience*. New York: HarperCollins.

Dewey, J. (1916) *Democracy and Education*. New York: Macmillan.

Green, R.L. (2001) *Practicing the Art of Leadership: A Problem-Based Approach to Implementing the ISLLC Standards*. Upper Saddle River, NJ: Merrill Prentice Hall.

Novak, J.M. (1999), 'Inviting criteria for democracy's schools', *Thresholds in Education*, 25 (1), 4–6.

Novak, J. M. and Purkey, W.W. (2001) *Invitational Education*. Bloomington, IN: Phi Delta Kappa.

Pirsig, R. (1992) *Lila: An Inquiry into Morals*. New York: Bantam.

Postman, N. and Weingartner, C. (1973) *The School Book*. New York: Delacorte Press.

Purkey, W. W. and Novak, J.M. (1996) *Inviting School Success: A Self-Concept Approach to Teaching, Learning, and Democratic Practice*. 3rd edn. Belmont, CA: Wadsworth.

10

■ ■ ■

Managing the Five Ps

Everyone and everything in schools should contribute to the success of
each student and to the quality of the life of the educational community. Inviting educational leaders work with people to design places,
policies, programmes and processes that systematically call forth
these possibilities.

How do educators stay alive in their work?

What is an imaginatively designed school setting?

How can programmes be more inclusive?

How can school change be approached collaboratively?

Because of the cohesion needed to hold a school together, these are
important questions for invitational leaders to ask as they seek to enjoy
and improve their schools. This chapter is *unlikely* to connect with your
beliefs if you:

- think professional development is a waste of time;
- believe that schools need to look institutional;
- feel that policies should come from the top down;
- think that schools need coercion to improve.

This chapter is more *likely* to connect with your beliefs if you:

- think a sense of vocation is important to educators;
- believe school buildings can be made user-friendly;

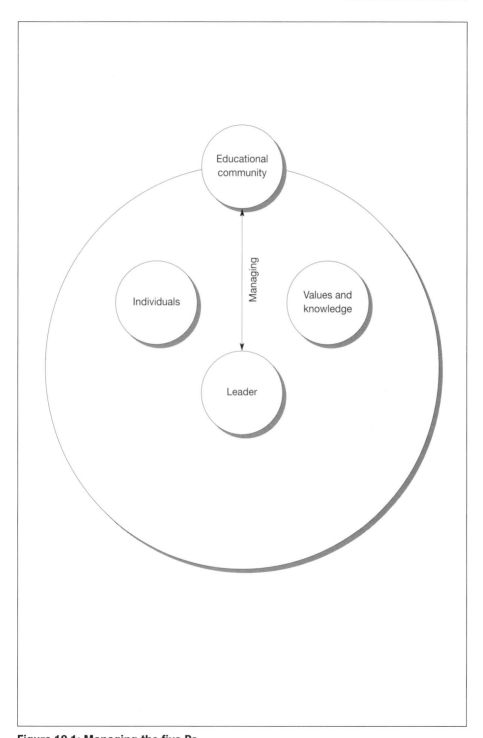

Figure 10.1: Managing the five Ps

- feel that policies can be collaboratively developed;
- think that people want to work in vibrant schools.

Just as everyone and everything in a hospital should invite health, everyone and everything in a school setting should promote thoughtful learning. This chapter looks at the five Ps of invitational education (people, places, policies, programmes and processes) and how they can be a part of an artfully orchestrated plan to make a school 'the most educationally inviting place in town'.

The five Ps

As an evolving theory of practice, invitational education aims to make a difference in schools. If the school ecosystem is made up of people, places, policies, programmes and processes, educational leaders can find ways to celebrate successes in these areas and apply steady and persistent pressure to make each area better. If each of the Ps can be thought of as a finger, people are the thumb that can point up or down. Let's look first at what people can do.

Beginning with people

Because invitational leadership is person-centred, it begins and ends with people. It is people who have to develop and sustain places, policies, programmes and processes. It is people who have to find identity and fulfilment through their engagement in schools.

Invitational leaders know that every person *in* the school is an emissary *for* the school, for good or ill. Nobody is neutral. To be neutral is to be apathetic and apathy communicates an empty spirit. Schools cannot run on empty spirits. The teachers, the administrators, the support staff, the custodians, the bus drivers, the secretaries, the librarians, the nurses, the assistants and the volunteers are all sending messages about the quality of educational life in the school. They are the thumbs, pointing up or down. If they are pointing sideways, they are trying to hitch a ride out of the school, and that tells you something about the quality of life there.

Inviting educational leadership depends on people creating, sustaining and enjoying positive interpersonal relationships. This positive tone is not based on a contrived congeniality, filled with fake enthusiasm and false smiles. That wears thin very quickly. Rather, a positive tone that can exist over an extended period of time depends on a sense of collegiality – a sense that comes from perceiving one's work partners as competent and well-intentioned (Sergiovanni, 1992). This sense that one's colleagues are doing the right thing in the right way for the right reason (and if not, it can be talked about) is what enables an educative community to sustain itself and flourish.

Places to care

It is hard to hide from places. They will not go away, even when you are hiding. Places are the sights, the sounds, the smells, the tangible totality our senses receive. These senses, however, can be dulled or put off by the institutional tone of a school or the lack of upkeep. Inviting educational leaders are aware of the powerful messages that are conveyed by the landscape and upkeep of a school and by the vibrancy of the school premises. They agree with Malcolm Gladwell (2000) that little things can make a difference, especially in regard to places. Citing the 'broken window theory' (p. 141), Gladwell points out that if a window is broken and left unrepaired, it sends the message that in this neighbourhood no one cares and no one is in charge. Soon more windows are broken and crime increases in the neighbourhood. This is the opposite of the tone intended in inviting schools: we all care and we all are in charge.

Perhaps this sense of intentionality comes across most tellingly in the messages communicated by the printed signs of a school. Signs say something about the tone and intent of a school. For example, a sign with the words: 'Visitors must report to the office' says something quite different from the sign: 'Welcome to our school. In order for us to serve you better, and for the safety of our students, please report to the office, which is this way →. Thank you.' The first sign gives more than information. It can be perceived as a harsh command by those who wish you were not there. The second sign can be perceived as a courteous greeting that conveys useful information along with a reason for what you are expected to do. The second sign is the type of sign you would expect to see in an inviting school. Several years ago I mentioned this to a group of North American principals and one became indignant. He said that in his state it was a state law that the first sign had to be posted. He asked me if I wanted him to break the law. Before I could respond, a second principal said that in his school he has both signs up. The inviting sign is on the top followed by the comment: 'The State

Department has not yet learned about inviting signs and requires that we post the following sign: visitors must report to the office'. What an impressive message this sign communicates.

Principled policies

Rules tell you about the rulers. In an inviting school that wants to prepare people to live a fulfilling life in a democracy, more and more people should be involved in formulating, implementing and evaluating the mission statement and the written and unwritten directives and codes used to regulate the ongoing functions of individuals and organisations. The sense of a school as an inviting educative community is positively affected by policies that are perceived as fair, inclusive, democratic and respectful.

Conversely, policies perceived as distant, irrational, exclusive or contradictory convey an oppressive, confused or out-of-touch way of operating. Attending to the process and product of developing inviting policies regarding attendance, grading, discipline, promotion and professional development is a key part of invitational leadership.

Curricular and extra-curricular programmes

It is important to analyse the intention and consequences of the formal and informal strategies that are established to meet the wide spectrum of needs of students. An inviting curriculum encourages active and meaningful engagement with others and the world of and for knowledge. If a programme is elitist, sexist, ethnocentric, racist, lacking in educational integrity or just not working, it needs to be changed or removed. The intention of inviting programmes are that they will help students live more educational lives. The outcomes aimed for should enable students to savour, understand and better more of their everyday experiences. Curricular and extra-curricular programmes must be examined with this end in mind.

Productive processes

This final P is concerned with the way the other four Ps are done. It looks at the tone, feel and flavour of the spirit of the school to the extent that it is democratic, collaborative and humane. By paying attention not only to what gets done (intended and unintended), but how it gets done, inviting educational leaders see how the process really is the product in the making. How we did something, and the consequences of what was done, live on in the habits and the memories of those who participated in the process and those who were affected by the product. Process-observing and improving is a very important part of inviting educational leadership. It is also a very important part of inviting change, which is based on a shared leadership process.

Inviting change

Inviting educational change is about more than one programme, or one method or one skill. It is about the artful orchestration of an evolving theory of practice, which is applied to real situations through the efforts of a diverse group of people with varying degrees of knowledge about and commitment to an inviting perspective. To aid in this process, educators have found it helpful to use the invitational helix (Purkey and Novak, 1993; 1996).

The invitational helix is a strategy for change that takes into consideration the different degrees of knowledge and commitment people and groups have regarding the inviting perspective. In terms of knowledge, the helix is based on the idea that people can possess awareness (they know about inviting education at this level), understanding (they know the important concepts of inviting education), application (they know how to start inviting practices) and adoption (they know how to sustain inviting practices) of the inviting approach. The commitment to an inviting perspective can vary from the occasional (enthusiastic renewal), to systematic (detailed application), to pervasive (extended leadership). Using these four stages of knowledge and three phases of interest, the helix presents a 12-step process for change (*see* Figure 10.2). Certainly educational change is more complex than this, but the helix can give educational leaders a structure for beginning the process. An artful orchestration process can develop from a simple beginning.

Occasional interest (Phase I)

Inviting educational leadership is a positive approach to appreciating and improving the good things educators are doing, along with pointing to other interesting things to try. By acknowledging current positive practices, inviting leadership builds on what people know how to do and

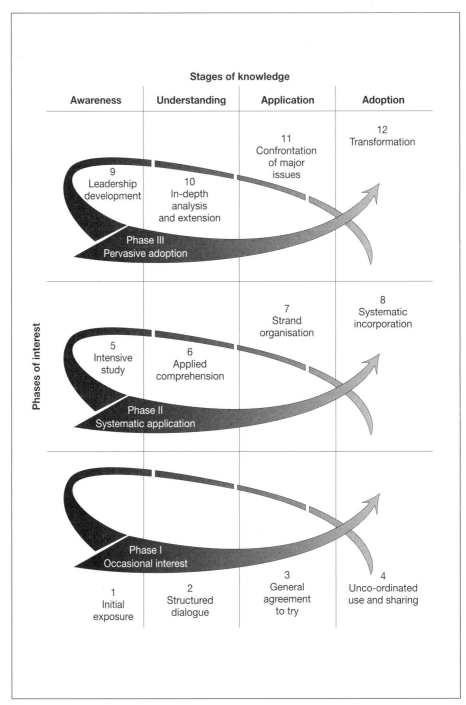

Figure 10.2: The invitational helix
(*Source*: Purkey and Novak, 1996)

help carry these into the future. During this phase, people return to their perceptions about why they came into education in the first place and how they can keep the spark alive. With much talk about teacher disenchantment with education, enthusiastic renewal can be a vital phase.

Initial exposure (Step 1)

People need to know about the inviting approach before they can do anything with it. This initial awareness can come about through introductory reading material, watching a videotape, attending a conference or visiting a school that practises invitational education. This initial presentation should be an enjoyable and provocative experience.

Structured dialogue (Step 2)

Building on the principle that meaningful learning is enhanced by social interaction, this initial understanding step involves organised discussion groups following a presentation, programme, speech or school meeting. As people discuss the basic ideas of invitational education, their present inviting practices are acknowledged. Group leaders ask why people think an idea is inviting in order to reflect on the idea of intentionality of practice.

General agreement to try (Step 3)

Invitations need to be put into practice to be invitations. At this step people agree to try a new idea or extend a previous practice. These actions may include cleaning up the school, creating inviting signs, reducing waiting time in the cafeteria lines or initiating a special-interest club.

Unco-ordinated use and sharing (Step 4)

Inviting educational leadership is based on a communicative approach to others, issues and projects. It needs to be shared to be appreciated and to get better. At this step individuals and groups report what is working and what is not yet working. There is a public recognition of successful new practices and people begin to think about the inviting approach at a deeper level.

Systematic application (Phase II)

Integrative change needs to follow individual and group successes. During this phase people work together for sustained periods of time and start thinking of the school as a whole rather than their limited territories. More structured approaches to transformation are put into practice.

Intensive study (Step 5)

As a theory of practice, invitational education is a series of interrelated principles, concepts, insights and strategies. At this deeper awareness step, the foundations, stance, levels and areas of application are explained by someone who has a solid background in the theory and practice of invitational education. A copy of the invitational model (*see* Figures 2.1, 2.2 and 2.3) can be used to explain the basic concepts.

Applied comprehension (Step 6)

A deeper understanding of the concepts of invitational education means that the abstract concepts can be related to issues that are taking place in the school. The questions regarding the inviting family school (*see* Chapter 9) may be discussed, relating them to people's current perception of the school. Those outside the group may be asked to share their perceptions of the school. A discussion within the group may follow.

Strand organisation (Step 7)

As a systematic method to brainstorm, evaluate and implement new practices, teams are organised into people, places, policies, programmes and processes strands. Employing a rotating procedure, each strand shares its goals, ways of proceeding, obstacles envisioned, ways of overcoming obstacles and methods of evaluation. A team leader is chosen for each strand and a priority of goals to pursue is agreed upon.

Systematic incorporation (Step 8)

Strands take on a life of their own by choosing names and logos. A strand leader schedules regular meetings and reports to and from a co-ordinating group. Reports are also made to the members of the school committee. Additional networks may also be established with other schools. A strand report form may be used (*see* Figure 10.3).

Pervasive adoption (Phase III)

At this advanced stage, invitational leadership permeates the educational community and becomes part of the deep culture of the school. The school goes out and provides leadership to other schools and systems. Following the idea that you learn something best when you have to teach it, individuals and schools make contributions to the inviting theory of practice.

Team leader _____ Team members _____

Team recorder _____ _____

Team energiser _____ _____

Team researcher _____ _____

Team focus: people, places, policies, programmes, processes (please circle one)

Specific activities and goals	Person(s) responsible	Time frame begin/end	Evaluation Success Measure

Figure 10.3: Strand report form

Leadership development (Step 9)

Emerging invitational leaders need to have not only know-how but also know-why. They need to be able to give principled reasons for why they made the choices they made. By examining issues and projects relating to the school from an inviting perspective, they develop an awareness of deeper possibilities and larger projects. New approaches to teaching, learning and leading are explored informally.

In-depth analysis and extension (Step 10)

To be knowledgeable about something is to be able to make distinctions that make a difference. Inviting educational leaders at this step can critically examine the inviting approach and compare and contrast it with other approaches. This critical perspective is used to examine and modify new initiatives according to criteria derived from invitational theory. That criteria includes the following (Purkey and Novak, 1996: 142):

- Is there a focus on a person's perceptions?
- Is there an emphasis on self-concept-as-learner?
- Will this initiative be humanely effective?
- Is this something we can do and not just talk about?
- Does the approach encourage democratic discussion?

Confrontation of major issues (Step 11)

The application of invitational education takes place within and outside the school. Members of the school are able to address key issues that affect both the school and the community. Groups outside the school share their perceptions and the school develops a deeper sense of purpose and practice. The idea of leading for educational lives takes on a deeper meaning.

Transformation (Step 12)

At this final step, invitational leadership is everywhere and permeates the whole school. The school, operating with an inviting family model, serves as an example of what schools can become. Members of the school present findings to other schools and conferences. Celebrations of success are everywhere. Living examples of this ideal in the USA include Calcium Primary School in Calcium, New York and Grand Island Senior High School in Grand Island, Nebraska. The approach is being introduced to the UK and is already being implemented in a systematic way in Hong Kong and South Africa. This book is an attempt to get things going. It really can happen.

Summary

- People, places, policies, programmes and processes can all work together to create an inviting school.
- All people in schools are educators.
- Collegiality involves working together to do good things in better ways.
- Inviting places send the message that people care and are responsible.
- The signs in a school are an indicator of care and imagination.
- Inviting policies are proactive and inclusive.
- An inviting programme encourages active and meaningful engagement.
- Inviting processes are collaborative, productive and humane.
- The invitational helix can be a guide to school transformation.

Extending the conversation

Q: Can focusing on the five Ps make a difference in an instituition as complex as a school?

A: The five Ps give educators a place to begin when looking at their schools. Rather than bemoaning the complexity of schools, the five Ps give educators a structure for inspecting and modifying what is happening in their schools. That's got to be of some value.

Q: Are the five Ps for teachers or administrators to develop?

A: Inviting educational leadership is about everyone in schools working together to make schools the most inviting place in town. This includes both teachers and administrators, plus staff, students, parents and community members.

Q: With all this talk about change in schools, don't you just have to get on with it?

A: What's 'it'? Inviting leadership is about doing educational things in educational ways. It should affect what is done in schools and why it is done this way. That's what we want to get on with.

Q: Don't zero-tolerance policies make it difficult to be inviting?

A: Taken literally, zero tolerance policies say there is no place for human judgement in deciding what to do. While I can understand the intention of such policies, this can be a mindless and spineless way of dealing with complex ethical issues. To attempt to do away with human judgement can prevent the development of ethical fitness.

Q: Isn't it easy to put good-sounding policies on paper?

A: It is not as easy as you may think. Many policies sound bureaucratic or extremely vague. Developing good policies on paper can be a helpful start. To paraphrase the old cliché, perhaps good policies have to be born twice – first on paper and then in practice.

Q: Isn't change more complex than what is presented in the invitational helix?

A: It certainly is. The helix is a guide for examining where a school is and where it might go next. The activities involved in implementing it have been tried in schools throughout the world. Think of the helix as a tool and use it with panache.

Q: You've not said anything for a while about a school's connection with the business world. Have you forgotten that?

A: Thanks for reminding me. That's where we are heading next.

References

Gladwell, M. (2000) *The Tipping Point: How Little Things Can Make a Big Difference*. Boston: Little, Brown and Company.

Purkey, W.W. and Novak, J.M. (1993) 'The invitational helix: A systematic guide for individual and organizational development', *Journal of Invitational Theory and Practice*, (2) 2, 59–67.

Purkey, W.W. and Novak, J.M. (1996) *Inviting School Success: A Self-Concept Approach to Teaching, Learning, and Democratic Practice*. 3rd edn. Belmont, CA: Wadsworth.

Sergiovanni, T.J. (1992) *Moral Leadership: Getting to the Heart of School Improvement*. San Francisco: Jossey-Bass.

11
■ ■ ■
Leading the
School Outside

> Invitational leaders are advocates for educational living within and outside their schools. They do not merely respond to the current societal forces but try to move these pressures towards educational ends in educational ways. Such efforts are necessary to help provide the care and ingenuity necessary for educational living to maintain, protect and enhance itself.
>
> *Where do schools end and the global society begin?*
> *To what extent should a school be in the community?*
> *To what extent should the community be in the school?*
> *What do we owe the future?*
> *How can the life outside the school be brought into the school?*

Because of the courage necessary to take the school outside and let the outside in, these are questions that educational leaders need to think about. This chapter is *unlikely* to connect with your beliefs if you:

- think that school doors can shut out the rest of the world;
- believe that any contact with the outside world will make the schools worse;
- feel that any contact with the outside world will make the schools better;
- think we need not think of what we owe the future.

This chapter is more *likely* to connect with your beliefs if you:

- think that schools and the global society are vitally linked;

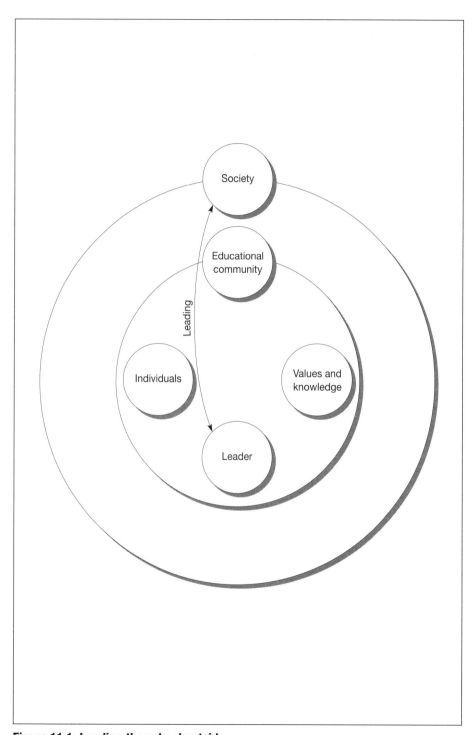

Figure 11.1: Leading the school outside

- believe that thoughtful contact with the world outside schools is possible;
- feel that educators have important responsibilities to the future;
- think that acting intelligently in the present is one of the best ways to prepare for the future.

Inviting educational leadership is about schools, and beyond schools, and back again to schools. It is about taking schools beyond their physical boundaries and bringing in the world outside schools. It is not neutral in its seeking educational ends for society through educational means. This chapter is about facing the larger issues that inform both school and society in terms of savouring, understanding and bettering the educational quality of life for all.

Ethical savouring in a global society

Inviting educational leadership is about seeking meaning and fulfilment in a real world – a world that will not go away even if we stop believing in it. The ability to savour life's experiences is dependent on the quality of relationships we have with life and the planet that sustains it.

Edmund O'Sullivan (1999) provocatively argues that there is a deep and serious problem regarding the survival of life itself in our present global structure. He contends that our modern, industrial, marketplace, competitive paradigm is a juggernaut that is increasingly destructive. Regarding this destruction, schools can either be part of the solution or part of the problem. Schools, he argues, can do one of three things:

1 *Business as usual*: bury one's head in the sand and assume the school is somehow immune from or not responsible for happenings in the outside world.
2 *Tinkering adjustments*: add a course here and there and have a few special activities during the school year.
3 *Radical reform*: transform the vision of what schools and education are about so that people can democratically stop the damage being done and move in a life-affirming direction.

If inviting educational leaders care about the human prospect during this intense period of possibility and peril we call the present, they will develop a reasoned and caring perspective on the relationship between their schools and larger global issues. Although, on the one hand, it is ethically irresponsible to avoid thinking about serious issues, on the other hand it is foolhardy to think that one's school can immediately attack all these issues.

Educational leaders can begin dealing with issues of global importance by looking at the working relationships their schools have with business and corporate groups. Inviting educational leaders can work to formulate a set of ethical principles by examining what other groups have done. For example, the following issues suggested by the Citizens Bank of Canada (2000), prompt some questions that need examination:

- *Human rights*. To what extent should our school do business with companies that have a poor human rights record or profit from child or prison labour? How do we know the companies with which we are dealing support international standards of human rights?

- *Employee relations*. To what extent should our school do business with companies that have poor records of employee health, safety, labour practices or employment equity? How can we tell if the company is a fair and equitable employer?

- *Military weapons*. To what extent should our school do business with companies involved with the manufacture of weapons of torture or mass destruction? How can we tell if a company is so involved?

- *Environment*. To what extent should our school do business with a company that has been shown to have a poor environmental record? How do we decide if a company has a progressive environmental record?

- *Treatment of animals*. To what extent should our school do business with companies that conduct tests on animals in the development of cosmetic, personal care or household products? How do we decide what is necessary research with animals?

- *Sustainable energy*. To what extent should our school do business with companies that are involved in the production of nuclear energy? How do we decide what is wise energy conservation?

- *Tobacco*. To what extent should our school do business with companies that manufacture tobacco products? How do we decide if a company derives significant revenue from tobacco-related production?

- *Business conduct*. To what extent does our school do business in an ethical way? How do we decide what ethical standards we should follow?

This list is only suggestive and does not stipulate what a particular school's policy should be. The point is, however, that inviting educational leaders have a commitment to the future of people being able to savour more of life's experiences. This future is affected by the state of the planet and the quality of life of its people and other living things. Inviting educational leadership is about maintaining, protecting and enhancing the conditions that make for a better quality of life for all people. The business and partnerships in which schools engage send a message regarding the values it believes are worth perpetuating. These are the values it lives by in the face of intense global realities. Certainly, these are complex and contentious issues, but ones that cannot be ignored by ethically responsible educators.

Understanding ingenuity in a global society

In Canary Wharf and the Isle of Dogs, capitalism has created a bewildering nightmare-scape of contradictions and mixed symbols that seem designed to distract people's senses and prevent reflection – designed, in other words, to substitute adrenaline, giantism, and raw audacity for subtlety, care, and reflection.

(Homer-Dixon, 2000: 79)

Perhaps Thomas Homer-Dixon overstates his case about a part of London and its symbolic effects. However, being committed to an ethical educational perspective that aims to enable people to savour more of their life experiences depends on a commitment to live life wide awake and to understand the complex relations people have with each other and the world. Certainly, there is an intrinsic value in understanding complex issues. There is also an important sense in which our survival may depend on how we adapt to the rapid changes we are making to the environment and ourselves. For, as Homer-Dixon notes, 'No matter how much we try to isolate or distract ourselves from reality, it has a way of intruding into the lives of even the smartest and most powerful among us' (2000: 80). How are inviting educational leaders to deal with these intrusions?

Homer-Dixon is concerned about the type of understanding we will need to solve the problems of the future. On the one hand, he is critical of those who think that the more rapidly we create problems, the more rapidly we will find better ways to solve them. This, he finds foolhardy and dangerous. The stakes are too high. On the other hand, he is critical of those who think that complex social and environmental issues will go away if people develop better feelings for each other and a sense of solidarity. For even if we are all in it together, he contends, we still have to use our complex understanding to work out how 'it' works. Both naïve economic optimism and romantic social solidarity leave out the importance of a deep understanding of the complexity of the environment in which we live. Both perspectives think it is all up to us. Homer-Dixon's approach to the understanding we need is to examine the requirement for, and supply of, ingenuity necessary to deal with the problems we are encountering and creating.

According to Homer-Dixon, the requirement for ingenuity is increasing rapidly because of the 'greater complexity, unpredictability, and pace of our world, and our rising demands on the human-made natural systems around us' (2000: 314). The supply of ingenuity is limited by the human brain, markets, scientific institutions and communication technologies, all of which can do some amazing things, but not all things.

It is wishful thinking to presume that we can easily supply all the ingenuity we need to deal with an often non-linear and complex world. There are 'unknown unknowns' – things that cannot be known in advance. There are environmental effects that we can only find out about after the fact. However, education involves sustained imaginative acts of hope that enable people to learn how to learn and get wiser in the process. In order to handle the possibilities and perils of our contemporary existence, and the unknown unknowns we will predictably face, educators can learn, for example, from what is necessary to survive in an aeroplane crisis when a non-linear system is wreaking havoc. Four factors, Homer-Dixon notes, enable people to have a better chance at survival:

- *Communication*. Having good interaction with others enables the right personnel and the right equipment to be available. Making sure there are secure communications links between key people is essential.

- *Preparation*. Doing the proper groundwork and being in a state of readied alert for what may happen helps reduce the odds for tragedy. Although there may be unknown unknowns, there are also known knowns.

- *Co-operation*. Making sure people can use their experiential knowledge helps them to problem solve. When a situation is not 'going by the book', it is important to have a group of people who know more than what is in the book.

- *Luck.* Since all the factors cannot be known in advance, success is not totally in our own hands. It helps if accidents happen at the right place and time.

Developing a mature culture of hopefulness (Slade, 2001) can be especially helpful in dealing with these four factors and thinking about the ingenuity that will be needed. Hope involves creatively and courageously dealing with situations that are not hopeless or clear-cut. With an energetic openness to positive possibilities, a wider horizon of meanings is available for problem solving. This wider horizon of meaning can include more thoughtful possibilities for both the supply and the demand sides of ingenuity.

Since the problems of an ingenuity gap are not only on the supply side but also on the demand side, it is necessary for educational leaders to examine the nature of the demands humans are making on the environment and our social-economic systems. This is especially true in terms of consumption. As Homer-Dixon notes, 'What we value as wealth and as the "good life" has an enormous effect on our need for ingenuity' (2000: 398).

Educational living is about being able to savour, understand and better more of our everyday experiences. This educational way of life is not dependent on hyperactive consumerism and a lack of care for the conditions necessary to sustain life. On the contrary, educational living is about taking the time and effort to learn to appreciate more of the life around us. It is about taking the time and effort to understand more about the world that supports this life. It is about taking the time and effort to act responsibly regarding how we influence all that partakes in this life. If this is what educational life is about, then educational leaders have to take the time and effort to make this a preferred way of living in the global community. Getting to peace with each other is a good place to start.

Bettering conflict

For the first time in history, we have the opportunity to shape in a conscious fashion our destiny as a species. Collectively, we can if we choose, issue a resounding 'No' to violence and coercion and an emphatic 'Yes' to coexistence and conflict resolution.

(Ury, 1999: 101)

Perhaps William Ury should read Homer-Dixon's *The Ingenuity Gap*. Perhaps not. Ury does, however, raise an important challenge: can we use what we know to prevent, resolve and contain destructive conflict, violence and war? Ury argues that the 'Knowledge Revolution offers us the most promising opportunity in ten thousand years to create a co-culture of coexistence, cooperation, and constructive conflict' (1999: 109). The development of this promising opportunity depends on people being able to think in terms of the 'third side'.

The third side, according to Ury, is 'the surrounding community, which serves as a *container* for any escalating conflict' (p. 7). Rather than thinking of a conflict as being comprised only of the two contesting parties, Ury proposes that we also see the importance of the role of the community. Community, looked at this way is '*people* – using a certain kind of *power* – the power of peers – from a certain *perspective* – of common ground – supporting a certain *process* – of dialogue and nonviolence – and aiming for a certain *product* – a "triple win"' (p. 14). Each of these dimensions can be examined from the perspective of inviting educational leadership.

- *People*: not some hierarchical power, but individuals representing the ethical will of the community to contain conflicts. In an inviting school culture, this would be all individuals who could address the conflicting parties from the perspective of what the escalation of their conflict is doing to the school they are all trying to build.

- *Power*: not the power of force but the force of persuasion that attempts to have the conflicting parties operate from the perspective of their interests and the group norms. In an inviting school culture, this could mean using a third person to participate in the 'rule of the six Cs' to return the conflict to a lower level concern.

- *Perspective*: not the power of one side over the other but the desire to appreciate the meaningfulness of each side's concern. Inviting educational leaders, working from the perceptual tradition, strive to have each person's point of view understood and to develop a larger shared perspective.

- *Process*: not only a concern for what outcome is arrived at, but also a concern for how the conflict is handled. Dialogue is the preferred mode. Inviting educational leaders work to have conflicting parties involved in doing-with (co-operative) rather than doing-to or doing-in (competitive) relationships.

- *Product*: not the triumph of one side over the other but the meeting of the needs of each party and the community. For inviting educational leaders this means helping to create outcomes in which people are able to invite themselves and others, personally and professionally.

For the third side to be employed in an optimal way, it needs to catch conflict before it escalates and becomes destructive. Preventing the negative is important in school and society. Perhaps more important, though, is how educational leaders pursue the positive in their relationship with the larger community. This is done through developing community connections and a deeper meaning of democracy.

Deepening democracy

Invitational leadership has a deep and abiding relationship with participative democracy. Participative democracy is an educative way of life in that it allows people to gain understanding and develop a more fulfilling character as a result of being meaningful constructors of a social order. As Stuhr (1993) notes, this participative way of life is an ethical way of being in the world and as such involves an ideal, cognitive and moral virtues, and a faith. Each of these requires some explanation.

- *Ideal*: not to be seen as something remote and unattainable, but rather something to be done – the active and imaginative union of the actual and the socially desirable.
- *Cognitive and moral virtues*: include what Wood (1992: 81) noted as the ability to think in terms of private interests and public goods; the commitment to learn from, but not be blinded by the past; the ability to enter public debate intelligently; the commitment to social justice; and a willingness to try new things.
- *Faith*: builds on the perspective of John Dewey (1916) of the possibility of the power of intelligence to imagine a future that is the projection of the desirable in the present, and to invent the instrumentalities of its realisation.

This deepening of an understanding of democracy is also a deepening of the foundations of invitational leadership and provides a more secure way to pursue valued social ends.

Leading the school outside means encountering many challenges: important ecological and social issues; the need to think about the supply and demand for ingenuity; ways to cultivate peace; and deeper meanings of democracy. Nobody said invitational leadership would be easy. It is, I hope, worthwhile.

Summary

- School and society are linked in concrete and tangible ways.
- Schools can strive to work with businesses that are committed to ethical practices.
- Schools are involved in the supply and demand for ingenuity.
- The ideal of educational living calls for an examination of our present way of life.
- Schools can help develop the people, power, perspective, process and product necessary for third-side thinking.
- In modelling third-side thinking, schools can help to prevent, resolve or contain destructive conflict.
- Deepening democracy is an ideal, a cognitive and moral virtue, and a faith.

Extending the conversation

Q: Isn't O'Sullivan's position too extreme to be dealt with in schools?

A: Educators need to examine what he is saying to see what validity there is for his position. If it lacks validity then they have learned something about the need for evidence in making such claims. If it has evidential support then to ignore it in schools is to turn our backs on vital issues of life and be guilty of educational malpractice.

Q: Are you taking an anti-market-society approach to education?

A: I think markets can be powerful and productive and powerful and destructive. It seems to me that rather than thinking of a 'market society' we should think of a society that can use markets for good purposes. To think otherwise is to think that everything in schools can be reduced to marketeering.

Q: How are schools going to get the money they need if they develop ethical guidelines for dealing with business interests?

A: If schools are to be about important educational purposes, they cannot just take the money and run. If educational leaders study their relationships with businesses and can defend what they did for educational purposes, then they are sending a powerful message about their school.

Q: The development of ingenuity seems so cognitive and technical. Isn't this at odds with the caring approach of the inviting family school?

A: The inviting family school is not anti-deep and anti-technical learning. That would be a very uncaring and escapist approach to education and life. The inviting family school is about learning important things that can promote the ideal of educational living. Learning to deal intelligently with the deep and serious issues we are facing in the twenty-first century is a vital part of educational living. Thinking through key issues of ingenuity theory is a way to go about doing this.

Q: How can schools fight the anti-educational trends of the larger society?

A: There are many trends going many ways in the global society. It is the job of schools to promote educational trends and to be critical of the anti-educational trends. With some imagination and persistence, schools can help start educational trends that live on both within and outside the school.

Q: You have only touched on some key points of the third-side approach to dealing with conflict. What else might we need to know?

A: The third side is a concept to get people to think beyond narrow self-interests. If schools can work to develop the virtues of this approach, then everyone who works in schools can become leaders in preventing, resolving and containing destructive conflict.

Q: Why is it necessary to have faith in democracy?

A: The faith that is mentioned here is a public advancement of meliorism. That is, a belief that there is a better chance that bad things can be made less bad and good things can be made better if we promote social intelligence and goodwill. This seems to me the type of faith that is necessary for a civil society to work and grow.

Q: Isn't this very idealistic?

A: Remember this book is about ideals that can be made manageable. The key test for educational leaders is to take these ideas and show how they can be sources of sustained imaginative acts of hope. That is what the next chapter is about.

References

Citizens Bank of Canada (2000) *Statement of Ethical Purpose*.

Dewey, J. (1916) *Democracy and Education*. New York: Macmillan.

Homer-Dixon, T. (2000) *The Ingenuity Gap*. New York: Alfred A. Knopf.

O'Sullivan, E. (1999) *Transformative Learning: Educational Vision for the 21st Century*. London: Zed Books.

Slade, P. (2001) *Habits of Hope: A Pragmatic Theory*. Nashville, TN: Vanderbilt University Press.

Stuhr, J.J. (1993) 'Democracy as a way of life' in Stuhr, J.J. (ed.) *Philosophy and the Reconstruction of Culture: Pragmatic Essays After Dewey*. Albany, NY: State University of New York Press, 37–58.

Ury, W. (1999) *Getting to Peace: Transforming Conflict at Home, at Work, and in the World*. New York: Viking.

Wood, G. (1992) *Schools That Work: America's Most Innovative Public Education Programs*. New York: Dutton.

12

■ ■ ■

Managing Democracy's Schools

Inviting educational leadership is about constructing a school culture that can maintain, protect and enhance an active democratic way of life. This means taking the school out into the community, bringing the community into the school, and modelling democratic governance.

How visible should the school be in the community?

In what ways can a school be democratic?

How can various groups work to create inviting schools?

How can the life inside the school be carried outside the school?

Because of the common vision necessary to manage schools for a democratic society, these are questions that educational leaders need to think about as they take their school outside its traditional boundaries. This chapter is *unlikely* to connect with your beliefs if you:

- think schools should be segregated from the outside world;
- believe that deliberation makes a school inefficient;
- feel that different groups cannot work to make schools better;
- think that democracy is merely about voting.

This chapter is more *likely* to connect with your beliefs if you:

- think that schools should extend themselves into the outside world;
- believe that deliberation is a fundamental part of getting an education;

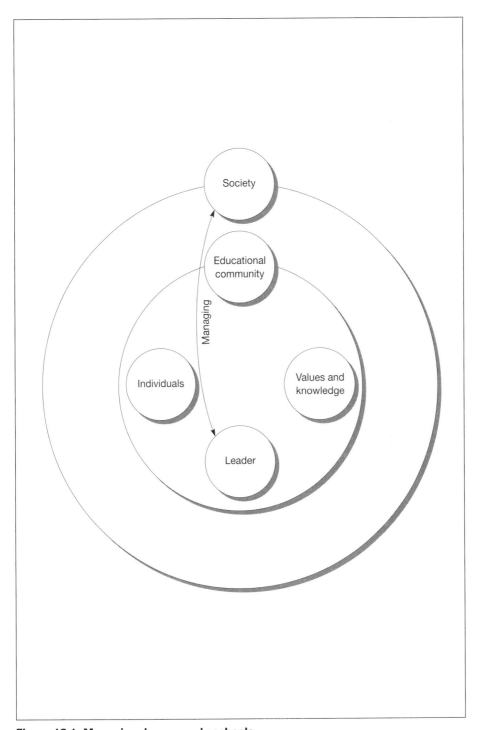

Figure 12.1: Managing democracy's schools

- feel that various groups need to work together to make schools better;
- think that democracy is a method of wisely developing social intelligence.

Amy Gutman (1987) has noted that democratic education is difficult because people want so many different things from their schools and their society. This chapter looks at some things educational leaders can do to take their message outside the school and creatively manage the diversity of demands put upon schools. The Inviting School Success Survey is used to involve those inside and outside the school.

Taking the school outside

Schools are known to the outside world by the messages they send. Intentionally inviting school leaders are proactive about the messages they send. They know their schools are known even before anyone steps through the door. Here are ten ways to communicate about your school to somebody new to the community:

- the local newspaper or neighbourhood newsletter has several articles about your school and its activities;
- you have a website that is colourful, informative and up-to-date;
- the local estate agents say positive things about the programmes in the school because they came to a lunch at the school at which the school's curricular and extra-curricular activities were explained;
- local stores and public buildings have displays of students' artwork and copies of the school newsletter;
- the school telephone is answered promptly and courteously and information is obtained quickly and efficiently;
- the signs on the school property are worded positively;
- the school grounds are clean and flowers are abundant;
- students are visible in the community and participate in a variety of social projects;
- the community is invited to the school for school fairs and other performances;
- the local television or radio station makes announcements about what is happening at the school.

These are signs that a school is energetic, welcoming and intentional. However, it is important that a school not rust on its laurels or just stay on the surface. Continual improvement is essential because if you stay where you are, the world will pass you by. It is important, therefore, not only to have enthusiastic renewal but also deeper application and appropriation of the inviting principles. This is a part of the larger ethical imperative embedded in democratic living.

Bringing in democratic practices

Inviting educational leadership takes seriously the challenge that a key purpose of schools in a democratic society is to prepare students to participate in their self-governance. Rather than students learning about democracy in the abstract, it is more powerful to let them see it in action, and even more powerful for them to be a part of it. It is also an important part of educating the community to witness and participate in the school's governance process.

Carl Glickman (1993), a proponent of site-based governance, points out that schools need three things to implement this approach: a covenant, charter and critical study process. Each of these can be looked at from an inviting perspective.

Covenant

The defining core values of a school can be seen in terms of the core values of invitational education (Purkey and Novak, 1996: 3):

- People are able, valuable and responsible and should be treated accordingly.
- Educating should be a collaborative and co-operative activity.
- The process is the product in the making.
- People possess untapped potential in all areas of worthwhile endeavour.
- This potential can best be realised by places, policies, programmes and processes specifically designed to invite development and by people who are intentionally inviting with themselves and others, personally and professionally.

This set of principles has been used by schools throughout the world in establishing their mission statements and covenants. We are only beginning to explore the depths of their possibilities.

Charter

The plans for putting into practice the core beliefs can focus on aligning the five Ps – people, places, policies, programmes and processes. Dr Kent Mann, Principal at Grand Island Senior High School in Grand Island, New York, uses a Building Leadership Teams (BLT) concept that consists of the following:

- Two co-chairs with a one- and two-year rotation.
- A steering committee of one person from each of the P teams with a one-year rotation.
- A voluntary faculty committee with a one-year commitment.

Operating with this structure, the school is so successful that it can run without the Principal. The charter has been internalised by the members of the school and has become part of the way things are done at the school.

Critical study process

The invitational helix can be used as a way to look at research and practice of teaching and learning and environmental effects on school climate. Through a variety of groupings of job-similar or job-diverse teams, people in schools can have regularly scheduled meetings to look at what is happening at their school, other schools and the world of research. The Building Leadership Teams at Grand Island Secondary School looked at student/staff safety, teacher morale and the personalisation of learning, among other things, in one school year.

Bringing the community inside

Moving towards more democratic governance and participation is a good start that gets better as the community becomes involved. To stay pro-active, schools can invite members of the community into the school to participate in an inviting evaluation of the school. This evaluation is formative in that it is used as an ongoing effort to make improvements. The community members are part of a team that can include teachers, students, staff, administrators and people from local agencies. The Inviting School Success (ISS) Survey can be used by the team as a discussion generator (*see* Figure 12.2).

The 50 items of the ISS Survey are broken into five categories, four of which relate to the self-concept-as-learner focus of the school, while the fifth category refers to the environment. The sections deal with:

- *Investing*: to what extent does the school encourage creativity and care?
- *Coping*: to what extent does the school help students succeed in a variety of things?
- *Asserting*: to what extent does the school help students have a sense of control over what happens at the school?
- *Relating*: to what extent does the school encourage co-operation and respect for everyone in the school?
- *Environment*: to what extent is the school clean and attractive?

The ISS Survey can be used as a heuristic for discussion. Each of the items could generate other possibilities that could be implemented in the school.

Invitational education can provide a philosophy and format for implementing shared governance. It must be admitted, however, that like any contract, the truth is in the details. The details referred to here are the degrees of commitment to sustaining imaginative acts of hope. These will be looked at in the next chapter.

Inviting School Success Survey

This survey is to give everybody in this school the opportunity to express feelings about this school.

For each of the following questions, please circle YES if you feel that YES is your answer, like this: (YES) NO ?

or, circle NO if you feel that NO is your answer, like this: YES (NO) ?

or, circle ? if you don't know the answer, or if you are undecided or if you can't say, like this: YES NO (?)

1   Does this school have a regularly published school newspaper?   YES NO ?

2   Are females and males in this school treated equally? YES NO ?

3   Do students have the freedom to talk with one another during classroom activities?   YES NO ?

4   Is music played in PE classes during indoor exercise periods?   YES NO ?

5   Does everyone in this school have a say in deciding school rules?   YES NO ?

6   Are people encouraged to begin new projects in this school?   YES NO ?

7   Do people who return to this school after an illness receive 'welcome back' notes?   YES NO ?

8   Do people in this school try to stop vandalism when they see it happening?   YES NO ?

9   Do teachers spend time after school with students who need extra help?   YES NO ?

10   Do people in this school offer suggestions on ways to improve the school?   YES NO ?

11   Are extra books available for use in classrooms?   YES NO ?

12   Do people in this school succeed in doing what is expected of them?   YES NO ?

Figure 12.2: The Inviting School Success Survey

(*Source*: W.W. Purkey, The University of North Carolina at Greensboro)

13 Are the grading practices in this school fair?   YES NO ?

14 Are comments made on returned homework and test
    papers mostly positive?   YES NO ?

15 Are people in this school on time for school and classes? YES NO ?

16 Does everyone in this school take responsibility for
    keeping the school clean?   YES NO ?

17 Do people in this school volunteer for special activities? YES NO ?

18 Do people in this school like to be here?   YES NO ?

19 Are most messages and notes sent home to parents
    favourable?   YES NO ?

20 Are people polite to each other in this school?   YES NO ?

21 Do people in this school make a special effort to help
    one another?   YES NO ?

22 Do people in this school express their feelings
    about things?   YES NO ?

23 Do people in this school have fun together?   YES NO ?

24 Are people in this school given important
    responsibilities?   YES NO ?

25 Do people defend this school and speak out in
    its favour?   YES NO ?

26 Are people in this school friendly?   YES NO ?

27 Do people in this school feel free to disagree with one
    another?   YES NO ?

28 Does everyone in this school know the school colours? YES NO ?

29 Does everyone in this school know the school motto? YES NO ?

30 Is special recognition given to each person on his or
    her birthday?   YES NO ?

31 Do people trust each other in this school?   YES NO ?

32 Are people greeted immediately when they enter an
    office in this school?   YES NO ?

33 Do people in this school know the names of many
    others?   YES NO ?

Figure 12.2: The Inviting School Success Survey (*continued*)

34	Are many nice things said about people in this school?	YES	NO	?
35	Is there a feeling of co-operation in this school?	YES	NO	?
36	Is everyone in this school treated with respect?	YES	NO	?
37	Are all the signs posted in and around this school positively worded?	YES	NO	?
38	Does everyone take a pride in this school?	YES	NO	?
39	Are the bulletin boards in this school attractive and up-to-date?	YES	NO	?
40	Do people like each other in this school?	YES	NO	?
41	Does the air smell fresh in this school?	YES	NO	?
42	Are there green plants in the entrance and hallways of this school?	YES	NO	?
43	Is the cafeteria a pleasant place to eat a good lunch?	YES	NO	?
44	Are the hallways and washrooms of this school clean?	YES	NO	?
45	Do the people who serve the food in the cafeteria wear attractive overalls?	YES	NO	?
46	Is there a salad bar for students and teachers in this school?	YES	NO	?
47	Is the lighting in this school adequate?	YES	NO	?
48	Are the walls in this school painted with bright colours?	YES	NO	?
49	Does the outside of this school look good?	YES	NO	?
50	Is this an intentionally inviting school?	YES	NO	?

Thank you for completing this survey.

I _____ Investing TOTAL _____

C _____ Coping _____

A _____ Asserting _____

R _____ Relating _____

E _____ Environment _____

Figure 12.2: The Inviting School Success Survey (*continued*)

Summary

- People should know good things about your school even before they visit it.
- Inviting schools are inclusive in their renewal projects.
- The basic assumptions of invitational education can be used to develop a school covenant.
- The five Ps can be used to implement a school charter.
- The Inviting School Success Survey can be used to make a critical study of the school.
- Shared governance can be modelled by the school for the larger community.

Extending the conversation

Q: Isn't it hard enough being an educator without having to have a presence in the community?

A: Your school has a presence in the community whether you like it or not. What is necessary now is having an intentional educational presence in the community.

Q: Shared governance sounds like a lot of detailed work that is best handled by others. Why should schools get involved with it?

A: Shared governance should not be about all the details of the school. It should be about the key educational issues of the school. That means it should be about central issues of teaching and learning and the five Ps.

Q: Covenant statements are usually just 'motherhood' pronouncements. How can we move beyond this?

A: The covenant is usually as good as the ideas of the people who really agree with it. To get a really agreeable covenant, you need to begin with some really agreeable ideas. My hope is that the inviting approach can be an important source of those agreeable ideas.

Q: What if not everyone wants to be involved in developing the five Ps?

A: Work with people who do want to be involved. It does not take a lot of people to become a critical mass and to get an idea to catch fire.

Q: How good is the Inviting School Success Survey?

A: It is only as good as the spirit with which it is undertaken. If it is used as a 'quick and dirty' method for giving schools a 'quick fix', then it will have limited, and possibly negative, effects. If it is entered into with a collegial and thoughtful manner, it can be the start of something better.

Q: What if the Inviting School Success Survey shows some negative things and members of the school community see this?

A: First, the members of the community will probably see a lot of very positive things and some current challenges. In a deeper sense, what the members of the community should also see is a school that is willing to seek to understand and improve itself. That is one of the messages that should make its way to the larger community – that the school does not want to rust on its laurels. Not letting the good get in the way of the better is an important aspect of inviting educational leadership.

Q: Do I have to agree with everything you said?

A: Of course not. I hope that this book has given you something to think about and some new ways to approach the important work of leading for educational life.

Q: Do you have anything else to say?

A: I thought I would use the last chapter for that.

References

Glickman, C.D. (1993) *Renewing America's Schools: A Guide for School-Based Action*. San Francisco: Jossey-Bass.

Gutman, A. (1987), *Democratic Education*. Princeton, NJ: Princeton University Press.

Purkey, W.W. and Novak, J.M. (1996) *Inviting School Success: A Self-Concept Approach to Teaching, Learning, and Democratic Practice*. 3rd edn. Belmont, CA: Wadsworth.

Part Three

∎ ∎ ∎

Dare to Lead
for Education

13

■ ■ ■

Sustaining Imaginative Acts of Hope

It takes persistence, resourcefulness and courage to orchestrate artfully the many dimensions of inviting educational leadership. Speaking the language of inviting can be a means to keep these ideas alive.

How can a mere mortal live up to all that is expected to invite educational leadership?

What questions might people have about the inviting approach?

How might the key ideas of inviting be summarised?

Is it possible to look at inviting as speaking a language?

Because of the hope that is necessary to sustain imaginative acts of inviting in education, these are questions that educators need to ask if they are to invite for the long run. This chapter is *unlikely* to connect with your beliefs if you:

- think it is too easy or too hard to lead for educational life;
- cannot think of any questions anyone might have about the inviting approach;
- feel the ideas are beyond summarising;
- are uninterested in speaking the language of inviting.

This chapter is more *likely* to connect with your beliefs if you:

- think leading for educational life can be an interesting challenge;
- have some further questions about the inviting approach;

- can think the gist of the approach can be summarised;
- are intrigued by the ideal of speaking the language of inviting.

This last chapter will bring together the key intentions of the Educational LIVES model by examining a crucial belief in each of the relationships: the leader within; individuals; values and knowledge; the educational community; and society and the other-than-human world. A way to speak the language of inviting will then be offered.

Sustaining educational LIVES

And if not now, when?

(Hillel)

The Educational LIVES model focuses on the quality of relationships in which people engage. These relationships can either call forth or shun human potential. The fulfilment of human potential is more likely to occur if people take to heart the following themes:

- *Leader within: care to live!* This is the belief that everyday life is worth living well. Through imaginative ethical living, each of us grows and can participate in the growth of others.
- *Individuals: share to grow!* In the process of learning to go beyond ourselves and connect with others, we construct vital relationships that deepen our appreciation for life and its possibilities.
- *Values and knowledge: compare to understand!* Approaching the world of and for knowledge in a disciplined and creative way enables us to see alternatives and make more informed judgements.
- *Educational communities: prepare to participate!* Education in a democratic society is about continuing and extending democratic ideas in people's life-work. We prepare for participation by means of participation.
- *Society and beyond: dare to lead!* The challenge of inviting educational leadership is to face the largest and smallest issues with an inviting stance. This involves being able to speak up for what goes on in the name of education.

Speaking up for invitational leadership

Invitational leaders will be called on to articulate their vision, in order to enroll participants within and outside the school. This is one of the tests of leadership. Leaders have a better chance of succeeding at this if they can demonstrate what Mortimer Adler (1991) calls logos, ethos and pathos. Let us examine each of these in terms of articulating the inviting perspective.

- *Logos*: the basic logic or cohesiveness of the ideas. The three foundations of invitational education, the stance, the four levels and the four dimensions can be summarised in the following 12 statements:

  1 Democratic ethos: extend the ideal that everyone matters.
  2 Perceptual tradition: look at behaviour from the inside out.
  3 Self-concept theory: see everyone as motivated.
  4 Inviting stance: seek to connect caringly.
  5 Intentionally disinviting: fight cruelty.
  6 Unintentionally disinviting: ignorance can hurt.
  7 Unintentionally inviting: being unreflective can be retrogressive.
  8 Intentionally inviting: mean what you do.
  9 Inviting oneself personally: keep your educational heart beating.
  10 Inviting others personally: support your support group.
  11 Inviting oneself professionally: stay alive in your vocation.
  12 Inviting others professionally: focus on self-concept-as-learner.

  The logic of these 12 statements centre around the idea that invitational leadership is about sustaining and extending imaginative acts of hope. Democracy as an ideal leads to an emphasis on the person and his or her hope for leading an educational life. An inviting stance is centred on care and aims to make a connection with another that is based on trust, respect, optimism and intentionality. Being intentional means doing things on purpose for purposes one can defend. If this approach is good enough to be used with others personally and professionally, it should be good enough to use with oneself, personally and professionally. As an evolving theory of educational practice based on a communicative ethic, it cares about what is taught and learned as we relate to ourselves, others, valued knowledge, educational institutions and the larger global society and beyond. Its goal is to provide the conditions so that greater numbers of people can savour, understand and better more of their experiences. And so it reconnects with the democratic educational ideal.

- *Ethos*: the creditability you have as a speaker. Your audience needs to know that you know what you are talking about regarding invitational leadership and that you are worth listening to. They need to see that your knowledge and insights come from both personal and professional experience. Your audience needs to believe that this is not merely something that you have taken from a textbook, but rather it is something you have thought about, studied, tried out, consistently lived and grown from. Sharing personal and professional stories that enable people to see and think about things they might have never considered before adds to your credibility.

- *Pathos*: the degree of passion and care you express. Your audience wants to know the extent to which you believe what you are saying about invitational education. Why do you care about this? What has it added to your life? Why should we really care about this and you? Pathos develops by showing people you own the idea and can speak about it from the inside out. Your audience should know that you care about inviting educational leadership and want them to consider caring about it also.

Meeting the requirements of logos, ethos and pathos, you should also prepare to respond to some of the key reasons people may give for choosing not to become involved with invitational education. Brown and Purkey (1999) in their research with teachers and administrators found the following six reasons (the basis for a reply is also suggested):

- *We are already inviting.* Reply: certainly good things are happening but without a systematic language to explain and extend this, there is the danger of rusting on your laurels.

- *It is just another bandwagon.* Reply: invitational education is part of a larger ethical project based on the ideal that every person matters and every way we do things matters. As a particular evolving theory of educational practice, invitational education has been around for more than 25 years.

- *It involves even more work than what we are presently doing.* Reply: done well, an inviting approach should save work. It is not an add-on but a way of rethinking what is being done now, why and with what results. This, plus the improvements that have been shown in discipline and morale (Purkey and Novak, 1996), should give people more time to do the things that are important.

- *It is an attempt to force change.* Reply: inviting is about establishing doing-with relationships. To force people to adopt this approach is to contradict its fundamental concepts.

- *It is too limited.* Reply: it is about orchestrating professional and personal behaviour with others and oneself and attending to people, places, policies, programmes and processes. Making all this work takes people beyond narrow purposes.

- *It is too 'feel good'*. Reply: feeling good is not a vice. However, people tend to feel better when they learn important things and are engaged in meaningful projects. Invitational education aims to have everyone wide awake and be able to savour, understand and better more of their experiences. This requires much deep and serious thought along with celebrations and playfulness.

Being able to answer these questions, along with the most difficult questions you can make up for yourself about inviting educational leadership, deepens your logos, ethos and pathos.

Inviting educational leadership and the seventh sense

We speak with words,
but they are not merely uttered,
they can be chosen.

We use a language,
but it is not merely words,
it is a way of being in the world.

We teach this way of being to others,
but they are not mere recipients,
they share with us their joys, hopes, and fears.

(Purkey and Novak, 1996)

In the film, *The Sixth Sense*, Haley Joel Osment announces that he can see dead people. Although this ability may make a good theme for the cinema, it is an inadequate perspective for inviting educational leaders. Their job is not to be spectators of death in an eerie world, but to be a source of life in a land of untapped potential. They need to possess the seventh sense – the ability to speak so that education can live.

Invitational leadership is about this seventh sense. It is about using a language of appreciation and transformation to call forth and sustain imaginative acts of hope. This book has been telling you about that language – about how to use it with yourself and others, personally and professionally. Perhaps a way to review that language and the subtleties, nuances and possibilities it opens is to see how it uses parts of speech. The eight parts of speech used in the inviting mood could be:

175

- *Prepositions*: work on 'doing with' and eliminate 'doing to' or 'doing in'. Prepositions represent the quality of relationships, the feel of how things are connected. Inviting educational leadership is about the delicate and precarious relationships that are necessary to connect people with themselves, others, values and knowledge, educational communities and social responsibility. Getting the relationship right at the beginning enables educators to move with intentionality and care in an affirming direction.

- *Nouns*: put people first, but also attend to places, programmes, policies and processes, along with ideals, ideas and adventures. Inviting educational leadership begins and ends with people. People are pivotal in the sending and receiving of messages. The other four Ps leave a symbolic residue that affects the behaviour, attitudes and values of those who come into contact with them. They are to be handled with an ethical imagination. Ideals are the imaginative projection of desirable present goods that enable us to move the actual towards the better. Ideas are vital to educational leaders who realise that anybody working with the transmission and transformation of ideas is doing intellectual work. Adventures just occur as people work to sustain imaginative acts of hope.

- *Verbs*: aim for the active voice and remember that 'invite' is a transitive verb and needs an object to complete its meaning. The active voice better represents a proactive stance. Invitations are always invitations to something. Educational invitations summon people to savour, understand and better more of their experiences. When in doubt about self-concept theory, remember the engineer Buckminster Fuller's statement, 'I seem to be a verb'. Each of us is a way of being in the world.

- *Pronouns*: employ inclusive forms and aim for 'we' rather than 'they', and go for 'thous' rather than 'its'. The 'we intention' is the ethical move to include more people in the circle of humanity. It comes about as one group is able to see more of the common humanity in others. Developing larger 'we intentions' enables people to use the 'third side' in social conflicts. Martin Buber's (1970) distinction between the 'I-thou' and the 'I-it' relationships says that the nature of the 'I' changes according to the way one relates to others. In an I-thou relationship I treat others as the centre of life and meaning. In an I-it relationship I treat others as objects to be used for my purposes. A more expansive, caring 'I' develops in 'I-thou'relationships.

- *Adjectives*: limit superlatives. Give 'best' a rest and find ways to use creative 'betters'. Taken literally the idea of 'do your best' can prevent some people from even trying or makes them go through prolonged procrastination. By thinking of the creative 'better' that comes from orchestrating skills and challenge, people can become more self-directing in their everyday behaviour.

- *Adverbs*: emphasise 'caringly', 'trustingly', 'intentionally', 'respectfully' and 'optimistically' to give the proper tone to verbs. These words direct the depth of our actions and enable us to dig in so that we can stand for something rather than fall for anything.

- *Interjections*: enjoy the 'wow!' and see 'gulp!' as an invitation to grow. Surprises, deeper understanding and feelings of competence are to be celebrated as vital educational experiences. The 'gulp' represents a felt difficulty into which we can enquire and work to integrate the new into the old as we restructure our web of beliefs accordingly.

- *Conjunctions*: focus on 'and' and avoid 'but'; use 'if' to help imagine possibilities. The 'and' and 'but' suggestion refers to the effect of using 'but' in the conferring stage of conflict resolution. Using the word 'if' puts us in the possibility mood and opens up the imagination to alternative ways of perceiving situations.

Learning to converse in the language of inviting with oneself and others, personally and professionally, is an imaginative act of hope. Just like learning any language, people will get better at it with practice. That practice can get even better as people become immersed in a setting where others naturally speak this language and create new possibilities with it. In such a place, that language can take on a life of its own and imaginative acts of hope become the norm. This book is an invitation to help create that place. May the conversation be extended to others.

References

Adler, M. (1991) *How to Speak, How to Listen*. New York: Simon and Schuster.

Brown, D. and Purkey, W.W. (1999) 'Reasons people give for not being inviting', *Journal of Invitational Theory and Practice*.

Buber, M. (1970) *I and Thou*. New York: Scribners.

Purkey, W.W. and Novak, J.M. (1996) *Inviting School Success: A Self-Concept Approach to Teaching, Learning, and Democratic Practice*. 3rd edn. Belmont, CA: Wadsworth.

Index

■ ■ ■